PRAISE FOR

7 LOVE LETTERS FROM *Jesus*

This book made me want to fall in love with Jesus even more. Throughout its pages, I was reminded of the unending love of God—a love that beckons us deeper and deeper into divine affections. A gift of a book.

MARGARET FEINBERG
Author of *The Sacred Echo* and *Scouting the Divine*

In *7 Love Letters from Jesus,* Rebecca Bauer provides a refreshingly practical and insightful approach to Jesus' messages to the seven churches in Revelation 2–3. She presents these letters as being warm with passion without being hot with anger (the latter often being the tone interpreters give this passage) and shows how they reveal the heartbeat of Jesus' loving summons to His Church. The depth of substance and richness of illustration that Rebecca provides—without trivializing the message of repentance in these letters—will make it a resource for pastors and teachers everywhere. Sound in interpretation, this book is accessible and solidly entrenched in the spirit of Jesus—that "simplicity that is in Christ" that will enrich and nourish any reader.

JACK W. HAYFORD
Chancellor, The King's University, Los Angeles
Founding Pastor, The Church On The Way

By weaving the story of her and Scott's courtship and marriage throughout the book, Rebecca Bauer brings a fresh perspective to the well-known letters to the seven churches found in Revelation 2–3. Her stories caused me to look at my own personal relationship with Jesus in a completely new light. I believe *7 Love Letters from Jesus* will help you rediscover what's most important—that God loves you—and inspire and challenge you to walk with Him in a deeper way.

ROBERT MORRIS
Senior Pastor, Gateway Church, Austin, Texas

Rebecca Bauer synthesizes personal pain, spiritual insight and theological revelation in a work that is sure to inspire, encourage and enrich your journey to the altar of the King of Glory. As you read these letters from our Lord, may you realize that He is writing to you as the object of His love and be open to receive the life-changing power of that love. You've got mail!

BISHOP KENNETH C. ULMER, D.MIN, PH.D.
Presiding Bishop, Macedonia International Bible Fellowship

REBECCA HAYFORD BAUER

7LOVE LETTERS FROM *Jesus*

PURSUED BY HIS LOVE
CAPTURED BY HIS GRACE

Regal

For more information and for special offers from Regal,
email us at subscribe@regalbooks.com

Published by Regal
From Gospel Light
Ventura, California, U.S.A.
www.regalbooks.com
Printed in the U.S.A.

Library of Congress Cataloging-in-Publication Data
Bauer, Rebecca Hayford.
7 love letters from Jesus : pursued by his love, captured by
his grace / Rebecca Bauer Hayford.
p. cm.
Includes bibliographical references and index.
ISBN 978-0-8307-6218-7 (trade paper : alk. paper)
1. Bible. N.T. Revelation II-III—Criticism, interpretation, etc.
2. Seven churches. I. Title.
BS2825.52.B38 2012
228'.06—dc23
2011045282

Rights for publishing this book outside the U.S.A. or in non-English languages are
administered by Gospel Light Worldwide, an international not-for-profit ministry.
For additional information, please visit www.glww.org, email info@glww.org, or write to
Gospel Light Worldwide, 1957 Eastman Avenue, Ventura, CA 93003, U.S.A.

To order copies of this book and other Regal products in bulk quantities,
please contact us at 1-800-446-7735.

To Scott

1954—2003

"All we do, all we say, all for Jesus, all the time."

QUOTE FROM A SERMON BY SCOTT BAUER,
OCTOBER 5, 1997.

DRAWING WAS A WEDDING GIFT FROM ARTIST
BOB ANDERSON, JULY 24, 1976.

Contents

FOREWORD
By Stormie Omartian

How often do you read a book where every page causes you to increasingly sense the love of God for you personally? This tender, beautifully written book by Rebecca Bauer does just that. In fact, it so powerfully brings home the reality of Jesus' love that—even as you are reading it—you know that the Holy Spirit must have directed and inspired the writing.

In this book, Rebecca helps us to see God's Word through His love rather than His judgment. She emphasizes that we need to see it from both angles, but that the perspective of God's love brings needed healing and peace to our souls. She has known love and has experienced loss, yet she has found that wonderful place of security in the love of Jesus that we all must find.

Rebecca brilliantly weaves her own love story throughout the book, from falling in love, getting engaged, planning a wedding, being married successfully for many years and raising children to the sudden death of her husband and how she learned to be complete in the Lord and His love regardless of the circumstances of her life. She beautifully relates her story to the seven letters Jesus wrote to the churches in the book of Revelation.

Even though this is more than a marriage book, anyone who is married (or contemplating getting married) should read it. I have been married for more than 38 years, and I gained valuable eye-opening insight from reading it. That's because the more you understand your love relationship with Jesus, the greater your understanding of how your relationship with, and commitment to, your husband or wife should be. You can better see the way marriage is intended to flow by understanding Jesus' steady and continuous love for His Bride, the Church, which includes all who believe in Him.

When Rebecca asked me if I would write the foreword for this book and told me what it was about, I said yes because she and I have been good friends for years and I trust her walk with the Lord and knowledge of Scripture implicitly. She hears from God, and I am always amazed at what He reveals to her.

The first time I met Rebecca, she was 16 years old. I had received the Lord in her father's office at the church, where a mutual friend had taken me to meet him during the lowest point in my life. Her father was the pastor, and everyone called him Pastor Jack. I started attending church there, and it became a lifeline to me.

Months later, after a Wednesday night service, I went to the little store at the church to buy a tape of one of her father's sermons. She was working there, and I was struck by her radiance as she waited on me. I was so impressed by her that I asked who she was and how long she had been going to that church. I was delighted to find out that she was Pastor Jack's daughter. She had a beauty that was remarkable, and I recognized immediately the loveliness of Jesus in her.

Three years after that time Rebecca was married, and she and her husband, Scott, became good friends with my husband and me. We spent many great dinners together during the years when we were all raising children. Rebecca is an excellent cook! By the time Scott eventually took over as the head pastor at our church, Rebecca had studied, trained, graduated Bible college and developed valuable spiritual depth, knowledge, insight and a tremendous ability to write. During those many years, Rebecca and her father and mother had an especially profound impact on my life.

She is still doing that.

With this book, Rebecca has touched me deeply, drawn me closer to the Lord, and helped me to further understand the depth of His love for me. It will do the same for you and for anyone who reads it. By the time you finish it, you will love God more, have greater appreciation for who He made you to be, and be better able to see yourself and those around you through the loving eyes of Jesus.

We all need to be overtaken by God's love in a fresh new way, and this book will gently sweep you along and into the arms of Jesus, where you will find the love of your life. Whether we realize it or not, this is where we all long to be.

Stormie Omartian

Bestselling author of more than 50 books with more than 15 million sold, including *The Power of a Praying Wife*, *The Power of a Praying Husband*, *The Power of a Praying Woman*, *The Power of a Praying Life*, *The Power of Prayer to Change Your Marriage*, *The Prayer that Changes Everything*, and *Just Enough Light for the Step I'm On*.

ACKNOWLEDGMENTS

Every idea begins with a seed sown by the Sower. I truly never cease to be amazed that when we ask the Lord to teach us about His Word, He starts sowing seeds in our hearts! It also never ceases to amaze me that He chooses to partner with us, so that the harvest always and only takes place with the help of many hands. I am so thankful for the many hands that He put in my life to bring this project about.

First, I would like to thank all of my children—Brian and Melissa, Kyle and Teresa, and James and Lindsey. Thank you for your prayer, your proofing, your suggestions and your encouragement. And thank you for releasing your stories to be told alongside mine.

To Kodua Galieti, Cordelia Kelsey and Linda Rand, who faithfully and patiently read, commented on and helped to refine the entire book: Thank you for your friendship and for your insightful reading of each chapter.

And to the entire team at Regal, especially Kim Bangs. Thank you for your availability, your encouraging words, and for believing in the concept of this project from the start.

HOW TO USE THIS BOOK

There's something that captivates our attention about weddings. The beauty. The flowers. The dresses. The antics of the ring bearer. The tears of parents who can't believe their baby has grown up. The radiant bride as she starts down the aisle, and the devotion of the bridegroom as he awaits his beloved.

More than simply enjoying the heart-stirring moment, though, I believe there is a reason we're so fascinated with weddings. It goes far beyond rejoicing in romance or wishing the happy ending always comes true.

Just as there is within each person an awareness of his or her need for God, there is also a desire—an innate longing—for an intimate relationship of love and trust. Many may find that longing fulfilled in a human relationship, but *all* of us can find that fulfillment in Jesus—our Bridegroom.

It's what He came for—to pursue His Bride and win her heart.

Your heart.

My heart.

Our hearts.

Does the thought of Jesus as a wooing suitor make you a little nervous? Don't be. He is the One who introduced this metaphor in Scripture. During His ministry on earth, He referred to Himself as the Bridegroom.[1] He's comfortable with that picture, because it's the only relationship that is capable of communicating the intensity of His love and passion for us.

This also means that we are now living in an engagement period, a waiting time; and there are some very practical "wedding preparations" that He calls us to. His love letters in Revelation 2-3 show us how we are to prepare and be constantly ready for His return.

So what are we supposed to be doing in the meantime?
How are we supposed to be getting ready?
And how can we know Him at this dimension?

I began to deeply consider this question when my three children were courting, engaged and getting married. They got married within three years of each other, and—wow—was there a lot of activity at our house! Planning notebooks, dress discussions, wedding showers, lots of smiles, lots of tears and a lot of growing up. It was all a part of getting ready to be married.

As I watched the swirl of activity surrounding their process, I couldn't help but make application to how we are to prepare for the second coming of Jesus. In fact, I've been thinking about that more and more. In the past several years of my life, I have discovered Jesus to be the faithful friend, lover and companion He promises to be. In this book, I hope to encourage this same relationship of Bride and Bridegroom between you and Jesus. To help accomplish that, you will find the following in each chapter:

- **The Seven Letters.** My whole life, I have heard the letters of Revelation preached about only from a negative standpoint—Jesus is correcting the Church. And He is very angry! Though there is correction taking place, that certainly doesn't tell the whole story of this portion of Scripture. These letters also give direction, declare love and look with expectancy toward the marriage supper of the Lamb. As we look at these letters together, I want to take a fresh look at them, focusing on the commendations of the Lord and how they correlate to wedding preparations so that we can be a Bride ready for His return.

- **Encountering Him.** These encounters appear at the end of each chapter and are designed to give you a tangible action point to apply each lesson to your own life. Throughout Scripture, God has given His people many action points. For example, water baptism is a picture of death and resurrection[2]; oil is a picture of healing[3]; the Lord's Table is a reminder of the price paid for our salvation.[4] In and of themselves, the water, oil, bread or wine have no power. It is our *obedience* to God's Word and our *faith* to claim something of its truth in our lives that makes the difference. I believe that action points are a kindness of God to His people;

He knows that we sometimes need something "tangible" to hold on to while we continually press forward in faith.

- **Love Letters.** As I prepared this book, I pulled out my own love letters from my husband and read through them. I learned so much about Jesus' love for me through the love of my husband that I decided to share excerpts with you. This certainly is not intended to hold us up as the perfect couple. Not at all. I simply wanted to share the joy of a healthy and happy relationship, as well as to illustrate, in yet another way, God's love for us.

- **Wedding Stories.** There are lots of wedding stories! Some are from my wedding, some from my children's weddings, some from encounters we've had over our years of ministry. While I've tried to use primarily "wedding" stories, I've also used some stories from my marriage. However, some of those stories cannot be told without alluding to how my marriage ended, with the death of my husband, Scott, in 2003. I only mention it here to put you at ease. God meets all of us in the dark times of life; but for me, it was in this season that I learned to meet Jesus as my Bridegroom. During His ministry here on earth, Jesus constantly illustrated His sermons with word pictures, fitting spiritual truth into a familiar and easily understood context. Similarly, many of our greatest spiritual lessons are learned simply in the course of daily living. Learning about Jesus as our Bridegroom can also be seen in our own culture's wedding traditions.

We're All the Bride

The very first step in this journey of encountering Jesus as the Bridegroom is accepting the fact that you—yes, *you*—are part of the Bride too!

What are your thoughts when you read that? Is it just something you give mental assent to as a nice figure of speech? It's in the Bible, so we believe it. But have you ever grappled with the fact that it actually means

you.

rebecca hayford bauer · www.regalbooks.com

I have discovered that large numbers of the Body of Christ don't know how to relate to Jesus as "Bridegroom." We have come to know Him as Healer, Savior, Lord, Provider, Comforter and even as Father or King.

But, Bridegroom?

That might be a tad uncomfortable for some.

Some may feel that by referring to Jesus in that way, we're somehow cheapening our relationship with Him—perhaps making Him "too familiar."

Let me reassure you that I'm not trying to diminish Jesus in any way. His call is always to intimacy and relationship; and it is with this word picture that He communicates how much He longs for that.

Others may not be able to relate to Him that way because their life experience on the topics of marriage and family have been negative. Thinking of Jesus as a Bridegroom could bring up a lot of past pain. If that is you, may I invite you to allow Him to become everything to you that people have not been? One of His titles revealed in Revelation is "Faithful and True."[5] Wherever faithfulness and truth have been betrayed in your life, He is present to heal and restore your heart.

I have also found that gender or marital status may make this a difficult concept for some. Even so, that statement stands.

We're all the Bride.

Before we go on, I would like to address those two groups—men and singles—who often wrestle with seeing themselves as "a Bride."

A Word to Men

I don't know what it feels like to be a man and have someone refer to you as "the Bride of Christ." The fact is, I actually was a bride; so thinking of myself in those terms isn't a stretch!

But let's be honest, gentlemen, the majority of scriptural metaphors describing what God calls us to be are very "male oriented." We are called to be a soldier, farmer, shepherd, fisherman, king, priest, athlete, father, son . . .

. . . and bride.[6]

I thought a man's opinion on the topic would be good, so I am going to share from a sermon by my husband and pastor:

I come to this morning's message with a certain amount of fear and trepidation. We're talking about families . . . and last week, we looked at them related to the personal development of our lives as individuals; that the family is not just comprised of moms and dads, husbands and wives, but of individuals who are being shaped into the likeness of Jesus.

Part of my trepidation in sharing is that there are a number of people who think, "He's gonna talk about husbands and wives today. I'm not one of those. I'm a single. I've never been married." And, there are others saying, "That doesn't apply to me, this wife stuff. I'm a guy."

Well . . . let me just ask a question . . .

Which one of us in this room is not a part of the Bride of Christ?

"Yeah, well," you might say, "that doesn't count! I mean, actually, I don't like to be referred to as that. For most of us guys . . . we don't like that! I wish I was 'the guy of Christ,' or 'the buddy of Christ,' or 'the co-worker or laborer for Jesus.' But part of the Bride . . . that's a little much."

But we are. We're part of the Bride.

We are being prepared spotlessly for His coming, when He will exercise His role as the heavenly Bridegroom, and we, the Church, submit to that leadership.

Which is the issue.

There are others who would say, "Well, you know . . . I'm not a father, I'm not a husband. I'm a single guy. I don't think maybe I'll ever be married; I feel comfortable and called to singleness. So why do I have to pay attention?"

By way of example, the apostle Paul wrote to "his son Timothy." Though not related by blood, Paul had accepted the role of model and mentor and man of God. As you accept that Jesus is doing something extraordinary in you as a man of God, people notice and say, "I want to be like you. I want to discover what you've discovered." All of a sudden you're fulfilling a fatherly role whether or not you have any genetic investment in the project.

So there are those who need to come to terms with that as we look at the roles of the people of God. Whether or not we accept those roles doesn't change the fact that there are people who relate to us in those fashions.[7]

Ultimately, of course, God's Word is for all of us.

We're all children—of our parents and of Father God. We're all called to fulfill mothering and fathering roles in the lives of young people around us. We're all called to work—we're all employers or employees, and the Bible calls us to give account in all of these roles.

And we're all the Bride of Christ. We're all called to come before Him in

> obedience
> > yieldedness
> > > trust
> > > > submission

While never compromising
> strength
> > leadership
> > > confidence.

Jesus lived perfectly—as a single, and as a strong man. He lived in authority—knowing who He was, and carrying out His mission. Yet He always submitted—"I only do what I see the Father do."[8] Though He lived a life of submission, Jesus' masculinity was never compromised. And yours won't be either. True submission requires strength. And true strength knows when to simply serve.[9] Life is always a balance of knowing when to lead and when to follow, when to move in authority and when to submit. Jesus lived a life that showed us how to do both.

A Word to Singles

The majority of my adult life has been spent as a married woman. In the years since my husband's death, however, I have learned a completely new understanding of what it means to live as a single person—in our culture and in the Church. I have also learned how faithful Jesus is to be the Bridegroom of one who is alone.[10]

Now that I'm living "singleness" up close and personal, I have discovered several things that singles struggle with when it comes to talking about marriage and family. First, I have discovered that they often view the idea of marriage from a viewpoint of fantasy, and they view "singleness" as a state of limbo—not developing their own lives, traditions or futures. This isn't a condemnation, nor is it intended to describe *every* unmarried person—I am stating generalities that I have observed.

Let me give you just one example. A girlfriend came over to visit one December evening. This woman is a bit older than me, but she has never been married and has no children. When she walked in the door of my home, she seemed surprised that I had everything decorated for Christmas. I presumed she just didn't have her Christmas tree put up yet, and asked her when she was going to do that.

She responded by saying, "I always thought that was something I would do when I got married; but that never happened, so I never put up a Christmas tree."

Then I got it. She thought that in my newly widowed state, I wouldn't do those things either. But I never got the memo that Christmas trees had a marital status! I challenged her, though. "Don't you think you're worth it? All by yourself . . . aren't *you* worth it?" The answer: Of course she is!

As I said, that's just one example. But let me state loud and clear: Singleness is not a state of limbo!

"Never been married" is only one reason people are single. Divorce is rampant in our culture; we all know this. But when Jesus shows up and says He will be the Bridegroom, it can unearth fear in the heart of one who has experienced that kind of betrayal and devastation—whether through the demise of his or her parents' marriage, or through the desertion of one who promised to love forever. And we so easily transmit the failings of human beings onto God, and fear that His promises won't stand either.

Yet "Bridegroom" is a metaphor Jesus uses about Himself, and Scripture offers a picture of what God's intention is for marriage. If your past involves divorce, set your fear aside when you come before Jesus. We're dealing with a different kind of Bridegroom now!

The other area I have observed that holds singles back from relating to Jesus as a husband is the susceptibility of viewing marriage, family and "finding the one" through a veil of fantasy. That is no one's fault. If you've never been married, how do you view the "reality" of it? Or if you grew up in a dysfunctional home, how do you know what marriage is supposed to be like? Our world today holds precious few healthy-functioning, spiritually solid, intact families. And, if you're waiting for a marriage relationship to come into your life, it's easy to imagine that "a perfect person" will come along. But expecting perfection will certainly limit your options.

Marriage and family are wonderful . . . but also a lot of work. Learning to live out our walk with the Lord as a couple in the nitty-gritty of daily life can become very difficult at times. When Scripture says that "iron sharpens iron," that other "iron" is likely to be your spouse!

We're all unfinished products. If we spend our time looking for perfection in anyone outside of Jesus, we will not only be disappointed, but we will also spend our lives chasing a figment of our imagination rather than stepping into partnership.

Unfortunately, we sometimes even treat Jesus the same way. He *is* perfect, but He never said life would be a rose-petal-strewn path. We blame Him, though, if life presents any kind of challenge. "*As long as You bless me, Jesus, as long as I'm healthy, as long as You do what I want You to do, as long as everything is going well . . . I'll stick around.*" As long as He's "perfect" and looks out for my comfort and doesn't challenge me, and lets me live in my fantasy of the "perfect Christian life"—I'll pray. I'll go to church. I'll serve Him. But when the going gets tough, people opt out of spiritual disciplines because Jesus isn't "doing the fantasy."

Jesus invites us to real life. But it costs. It costs letting go of the fantasy and growing into partnership with Him. It costs confronting the fear in your own life that keeps you from commitment, vulnerability and accountability. It challenges your comfort zone, calls you to growth, drives you to complete dependence on Him, and cultivates in you the character traits that make you as real as He is.

Despite the work that a relationship requires, the Bible tells us that while one shall put a thousand to flight, "two [shall] put ten thousand to flight"[11] and that "two are better than one."[12] Together, our efforts are multiplied. But it doesn't come without a whole lot of falling on your face in prayer, laying down your "rights," saying you're sorry, submitting to the Lord, seeking to serve Him at all times, and seeking the best for each other. When you're *both* doing that—when you're *both* living that way—marriage is one of the most amazing experiences in the world.

I say all of that to point out that our tendency as single people (and I include myself here) is to think that marriage is somehow "better." We tend to view married life through unrealistic rose-colored glasses—or to imagine it's just all romance, flowers and candy every night. This view doesn't allow us to come completely to Jesus as our husband.

Jesus does love us. In fact, He's passionate about us! But He is also committed to bringing us to our potential. He is also committed to seeing freedom brought into our lives. He is also committed to confronting bad attitudes in us. All are marks of a truly excellent husband! If we are unprepared for that aspect of "marriage" as the Bride of the Lamb, we miss a large part of what He desires to do in us—not just as our Savior, not just as our Lord . . . but as our Bridegroom.

As we begin this journey together . . . *you* are part of the Bride! Jesus wants to woo you. He wants to pursue your heart like an ardent Lover, with a passion that is all consuming! Wherever you find yourself today—regardless of gender or marital status, social status or how long you've walked with Jesus—

you are part of the Bride.

---

1. See Matthew 9:15 and 25:1-13.
2. See Romans 6:4.
3. See James 5:14.
4. See 1 Corinthians 11:26.
5. See Revelation 19:11.
6. See 2 Timothy 2:3; Matthew 9:38; 1 Peter 5:2; Mark 1:17; Revelation 1:6; 1 Corinthians 9:24; Philippians 2:22; 1 John 3:1.
7. From a sermon preached on October 12, 1997. If you are interested in listening to this entire sermon, it may be accessed at www.rebeccabauer.org.
8. See John 5:19.
9. See Mark 10:44.
10. See Isaiah 54:5.
11. Deuteronomy 32:30.
12. Ecclesiastes 4:9.

Prologue

LOVE LETTERS

Scott and I met at church.

Where else? And to this day I could take you to the spot where his sister Susan introduced us.

I even wrote it in my diary. Yep . . . I was pretty impressed.

Scott was impressed too! That was easy enough to see. But this was a season in his walk with the Lord where he felt that he wasn't to pursue a dating relationship with anyone. So we remained friends for many months before we ever went out. At church, I often sat with Susan, and *amazingly*, Scott decided to sit with her too. (I mean, really, who sits with his sister? He obviously had an ulterior motive!) It was in this time that we began to get to know each other—before, during and after church services.

During? Well . . . yes. I would have to say that our first "love letters" were written on the backs of prayer request cards and passed during church services! That may not seem like much of a love letter to you, but that is what they were. They weren't great declarations of passion, nor were they particularly profound. They were seemingly trivial comments that two hearts longing to communicate with each other just couldn't wait to say until after church!

> *What are you doing this week?*
> *How did your final exam go?*
> *What days will you be working?*
> *Will you be at church Wednesday?*

> Pretty general, yes, but love letters just the same. It was in that season
> while friendship grew,
> while we were getting to know each other,
> while we were growing in the Lord together,
> that *love blossomed.*

And eventually, one of the love notes asked me out for a date. I said yes.

I followed up our first date with a love letter. I didn't know it was a love letter at the time. It wasn't intended to be one. It was intended to be a simple thank-you, but it had long-term ramifications.

According to Scott, our first date was a dismal failure. He was a student at UCLA and had been given two tickets to a student production. We went—and then left early at Scott's insistence. He was shocked and embarrassed at all the double entendre in the script. And me? I was too naïve to even recognize it. He told me later that he'd been so humiliated by the experience that he had actually decided to never ask me out again.

But then he got my note and changed his mind.

A simple thank-you note

A card

A love letter

Hurray for love letters!

Twenty-six years later, Scott was still referencing that thank-you note! The front of my Valentine that year read: "It was a nudge, a hunch, a funny feeling that something very special was about to happen . . ." Inside he wrote:

Do people still write love letters?

In our high-tech cyber-era, maybe the "new" love letter is an email, a text, a post, a tweet or an animated online card.

In my opinion, however, nothing quite replaces the thrill of seeing your beloved's handwriting. His (or her) signature. A letter in the mail that is just for *you!* Call me old-fashioned, but an email can be too easily forwarded; a text can be erased; an e-card accidentally sent to junk mail.

But a letter is tangible. It can be carried, read until it is worn and creased, put under a pillow, held to your heart, tied with a ribbon and treasured. There's just something about a love letter . . .

> It invites response
>> reawakens memories
>>> woos your heart
>>>> and affirms again and again that . . .
>>>>> *You are loved!*

You've Got Mail

What if Jesus wrote you a love letter?

Would you treasure it? Would you keep it close by? Would you read it and reread it? He has written you a love letter, you know. Of course, I'm talking about the Bible. It reveals God's heart for us.

> *For God so loved . . .*
> *Abide in My love.*
> *[Nothing] shall be able to separate us from the love of God.*
> *He first loved us.*[1]

Too often, though, we don't view Scripture as a love letter. In fact, this book you're holding was inspired by just that thought—that we as imperfect people generally focus on the "corrections and disciplines" of Scripture rather than on what is revealed of God's heart.

And His love is evident everywhere in His Word!

From the paradise He originally created for humankind in Genesis, to the redemption of Jesus Christ on the cross, to the home He is preparing for us in Revelation, the fact is

> *He loves us!*

The New Testament doesn't tell us whether the apostle Paul was ever married or not. Whatever the case may be, he understood that marriage was to parallel the love Jesus has for His church. Paul describes the relationship of a committed couple with tenderness and beauty.[2] He writes that husbands are to love their wives as Christ loves the Church and that wives are to yield to their husbands just as the Church yields to Christ. It's a relationship based completely on love and sacrifice. As such, it harms no one but builds everyone. It is the same kind of relationship that Jesus desires to have with us. That may sound scary to some, but look at how God defines love:

> *Love never gives up.*
> *Love cares more for others than for self.*
> *Love doesn't want what it doesn't have.*
> *Love doesn't strut,*
> *Doesn't have a swelled head,*
> *Doesn't force itself on others,*
> *Isn't always "me first,"*
> *Doesn't fly off the handle,*
> *Doesn't keep score of the sins of others,*
> *Doesn't revel when others grovel,*
> *Takes pleasure in the flowering of truth,*
> *Puts up with anything,*
> *Trusts God always,*
> *Always looks for the best,*
> *Never looks back,*
> *But keeps going to the end.*[3]

Make no mistake, 1 Corinthians 13 isn't just a nice chapter to read at weddings. It's not just a sappy, unrealistic fairy tale. It's not Don Quixote singing "The Impossible Dream." This is how God commits to us.

Can I say that again? This is how God commits to us.

    Love gives

        Love sees potential

            Love desires the best for the beloved

                Love pursues.

When we talk about Jesus' love for us, we have to have our own minds transformed to look at love by His definition.

Giving. Pursuing. Longing. Wooing. Staying.

Jesus isn't "in this" for what He can get out of us. He wants to pour His love on us; He longs to bring us into relationship with Him. We are His beloved! So let me ask again . . .

What if Jesus wrote you a love letter?

As we go through this book, I want you to look at seven love letters He has written to His church . . . His bride—us. The letters to the churches in Revelation, I believe, are love letters to us, the Bride, to prepare us for the coming of the Bridegroom. "Revelation" literally means "unveiling"; and John describes his vision as the "revelation of Jesus Christ." While many use the book of Revelation to speculate about end times, it is intended to unveil Jesus to us in a new way—as our Bridegroom. The book ends with Jesus coming for His Bride, and with the marriage supper of the Lamb. So it only seems logical that the book would begin with love letters and an invitation to prepare for the coming of the Bridegroom.

Rise up, my love, my fair one, and come away.[4]

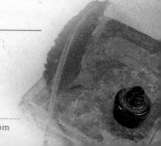

1. John 3:16; John 15:10; Romans 8:39; 1 John 4:19.
2. See Ephesians 5:22-23.
3. 1 Corinthians 13:3-7, *THE MESSAGE*.
4. Song of Songs 2:10.

Encountering Him

MIRROR, MIRROR

Part of accepting Jesus as our Bridegroom requires that we accept ourselves as part of the Bride . . . to see ourselves as Jesus sees us. We see all of our imperfections, but He looks beyond to our potential. I learned a different way of seeing not only myself but also the heart of Jesus through the love of my husband.

I met my earthly bridegroom when I was only 17 years old, and we married two years later. Like many teenage girls, my opinion of myself—my worth, my self-esteem—was not particularly high. I was hesitant, apologetic, reserved, fearful. Yet somehow, Scott saw beyond that to the core of my being that was focused, goal-oriented and passionately in love with Jesus. He liked that about me, and it became his lifelong mission to see that what was on the inside of me became visible on the outside. He saw my potential and was committed to its development. Scott believed that I could accomplish anything. He longed for me to see myself though the eyes of his love for me—to see myself as he saw me.

One of the first—and sweetest—lessons that I learned took place during our first year of marriage. Every morning when we first woke up, Scott would look at me and say, "You're beautiful!" Of course, I didn't believe him; but over time, Scott's words began to penetrate, and my perspective changed. In part, I learned to see myself with Scott's eyes in front of the mirror. (And I won't deny that there were a few combs thrown at that mirror! These are hard lessons to learn.) Eventually, I did begin to see myself with Scott's eyes; and in the process, I learned some very powerful lessons about Jesus, and how He saw me.

- Jesus, too, saw all of my potential and was fully committed to seeing that developed in me.
- Jesus is more interested in me than in what I can produce for Him.
- Jesus is more concerned about my welfare than He is about His own. (It's why He was willing to die for me.)

- Jesus will always tell me the truth; I can trust Him completely, and He will never leave me nor forsake me.
- No matter what is happening, Jesus is a safe place to go.

Having learned these lessons, I gave a similar assignment to a group I was teaching. Each person was to go home and look in the mirror. As they looked, they were to meet their own eyes and say, "Jesus loves me." I got some very interesting responses when I gave the assignment!

- "I don't look in mirrors."
- "I never wear my glasses when I look in the mirror . . . that way, I don't see the wrinkles."
- "I only see what's wrong when I look in the mirror."

Several refused to do the assignment at all.

The majority of us have difficulty looking at ourselves in a mirror and seeing what's good. After all, we usually go to a mirror to find out what needs to be fixed! Few of us are there just to admire ourselves. But I'm going to give you the assignment anyway. Go to a mirror, look yourself in the eye and say,

I'm the Bride.

We are each learning to see ourselves through Jesus' eyes, with all of the beauty, potential and uniqueness that make each one of us who *we are*. I won't pretend this is easy.

Scott was once asked to speak to a women's group. The day before he spoke, the Lord showed him a mental picture of women putting on their makeup and getting dressed up to go somewhere special—but they were doing it in front of a fun house mirror. That kind of mirror is created to distort and confuse what it reflects. Yet, here were all of these women putting on makeup until it looked "normal" within a distorted mirror. Of course, when they stepped away from the mirror, the distortion of their makeup was evident to everyone around them. They had prepared themselves in front of a mirror that lied to them.

The next day, he shared that word-picture with the ladies present and challenged them to confront the things that lie to them—rejection, low self-esteem, fashion magazines, 10 extra pounds, whatever it is—and step in front of the clear, pure reflection of what God's Word says about us.

So what does God say?

The King will greatly desire your beauty;
Because He is your Lord, worship Him....
The royal daughter is all glorious within the palace;
Her clothing is woven with gold.
She shall be brought to the King in robes of many colors.[1]

Behold, you are fair, my love! Behold, you are fair!
You have dove's eyes behind your veil....
Who is she who looks forth as the morning,
Fair as the moon, clear as the sun,
Awesome as an army with banners?
How fair and how pleasant you are, O love, with your delights![2]

The Bible also says that "we all, with unveiled face, beholding as in a mirror the glory of the Lord, are being transformed *into the same image* from glory to glory, just as by the Spirit of the Lord."[3] Can you imagine? When God looks at us, He sees . . . Jesus. And He whispers to each of us

You are beloved.

You are beautiful.

You are the Bride.

Love Letter

The passion of a thousand lovers,
The joy of a thousand bridegrooms,
The security of being encompassed by the heavenly host,
The peace of a lazy summer day
The pride of a brand-new father
And the wonder of a man who asks . . . why me?

sgb to rlb
Valentine's Day, 1981

1. Psalm 45:11,13.
2. Song of Songs 4:1; 6:10; 7:6.
3. 2 Corinthians 3:18 (emphasis added).

FIRST COMES LOVE

The extended Bauer family celebrated nine weddings in eight years—those of nieces, nephews and my own three children. The family aspect of these events could never be overstated. The weddings gave us an annual built-in excuse to have giant, exciting family reunions. We had a blast!

If there is one thing I learned throughout that time, though, it was that preparing for a wedding is no small project! Every detail counts—from ribbons (and how they are tied), to special shoes, to lipstick color. Invitations, cakes and caterers, dresses and DJs . . . there are a lot of details that go into the process! One of our brides even made sure to use teeth whitening strips so that her smile would be as radiant as she was on her wedding day!

As surely as there is a process in planning a wedding, there is also a process in moving toward marriage. Each stage of a relationship, from first introduction to wedding reception, has a purpose in establishing the solid foundation for the couple to begin their life together. In fact, when the apostle John describes the new Jerusalem, identifying it as "the Lamb's wife," he says that the city has 12 foundations.[1]

While we may not pour 12 foundations when preparing for a wedding, there are steps to making sure that the support structure of a relationship is secure, solid and can stand the test of time. Each step of the process counts; each phase has a purpose.

Before I Knew You

Viewed from our side as parents, the process of marrying off our kids began long before the wedding. In fact, it actually started at birth. From the time when each of our children was born, we prayed for their mates—knowing that "somewhere out there," those people were already in existence and God knew who they were.

It moves me beyond measure to think that when Melissa was 7, and she was trying to deal with the collapse of her parents' marriage, we were praying for her; when Teresa was 11, and her parents moved to the

United States to find a better life for their family, we were praying for her; when James was 12, and his family home caught fire, we were praying for him. We prayed for them before we knew them.

Healing. Provision. Opportunity. Hope. Protection.

Prayer was the foundation from which we progressed. As our children grew, we were very intentional in talking to them about marriage—the covenant that it is, how one chooses a mate, and what one looks for. They needed to understand the importance of family—extended family, loyalty to siblings, honoring parents, and accepting the family of one's spouse. All of these were discussed and lived out in front of them as Scott and I processed our own marriage.

But we also wanted to help our children learn the "why" behind how we lived, how they were being raised, how relationships worked and how it all tied back in to Scripture. That isn't to say that we had Tuesday night classes at home called "Marriage 101." We dealt with issues as they came up in the course of living, and we were intentional about not letting those moments pass.

Deuteronomy 6 talks about those kinds of moments. While it's a text that challenges parents to teach their children, it should be a part of every believer's life—living and learning about God's Word, all of the time.

> *You shall . . . talk of them*
> *when you sit in your house, when you walk by the way,*
> *when you lie down, and when you rise up.*
> *You shall bind them . . . on your hand,*
> *and they shall be as frontlets between your eyes.*
> *You shall write them on the doorposts of your house.*[2]

This doesn't mean you have to have a Scripture ready for every occasion, or have Bible verse wall plaques all over the house. It *does* mean to watch for the teaching moments of life so that values, principles and beliefs can be transmitted to the next generation in a practical, hands-on way. It took time to talk about all of those things. It wasn't convenient to stop what we were doing and address something at the moment it came up. It took intention and commitment; but it was worth it. All of our children have chosen very well in marriage.

Finishing Touches

Once they were engaged, there were issues that Scott addressed with our sons. We had laid the groundwork, and now it was time for finishing touches. It was time to help "college boys in love" think like "men about to start families." Our sons were engaged at the same time, and both were still living at home. Issues came up. And as I said, we didn't let those moments slip by. Scott specifically talked with Brian and Kyle about ways to think in taking on the responsibilities of a man. I remember hearing conversations on these topics:

- *Living as people of faith.* We live responsibly, but we don't make decisions based on fear. We base our decisions on God's Word and what we believe.
- *Financial issues.*
- *Keeping the priority of the beloved,* and learning to choose the things that are best for "us as a couple" rather than just "me as an individual."
- *Good communication.* How do you honor each other in how you disagree . . . and how do you resolve issues?

These lessons are true for girls, too, but Scott had already gone to be with the Lord by the time Lindsey got married.

Which made her process immensely different.

Of course, there were some very poignant moments for both of us as we walked the process without Scott. I took over in putting on the "finishing touches." We talked about the same things Scott had talked to our sons about. But Lindsey had one big additional question to process:

How can I appropriately honor my dad at my wedding?

She was firm in her decision to have her dad be part of her day. "Dad knew James and approved of him!" she said. But finding the balance of including Scott in an honoring way without making the moment gloomy was at times an emotionally harrowing experience. One of the questions we had to answer was deciding who would walk her down the aisle. She decided on Grandpa Bauer—her dad's dad.

Which brought up another poignant memory.

Scott used to walk Lindsey down the long hallway in our house, arm in arm, so they could "practice" for this future event. Those moments turned out to be a sweet kindness of God to my daughter. She knew what it felt like to walk down the aisle (okay—hallway) with her dad.

Early on in Lindsey's process, however, I also discovered that dads ask potential grooms entirely different questions than moms do. So I figured out a way to make up the difference on that point. When it became clear that a proposal was near at hand, I gave James a process. I asked him to talk to three men that are a part of our family's life: my dad (older generation of the family), my brother-in-law (same generation as Scott and me), and our pastor. When all of *that* was completed, James could ask *me* for Lindsey's hand in marriage, and *then* he could propose.

Whew!

James was amazing. He still is! But in that season, I came to deeply appreciate the level of character in the man my daughter had chosen. He and Lindsey were dating when Scott died. It was obvious, though, where this relationship was headed—Scott had already started a wedding fund.

When Scott passed away, James "slowed down the relationship." He told Lindsey that he wanted to give her time to process her loss, and he didn't want her saying yes to an engagement because she was trying to fill something in her heart. Otherwise, I think they would have been engaged months sooner. At any rate, James was there to walk through the grief with Lindsey; but he waited to move the relationship past "dating." Pretty mature for a 20-year-old.

Now I was asking him to meet with all of these people. He readily agreed. I wasn't trying to be mean, but I was trying to make sure that all of the bases were covered. I wanted to make sure that the foundation was secure. I wanted to know that everything was in place for the greatest likelihood of success and the easiest possible transition to married life.

In our family's season of many engagements and weddings, one of the most important lessons I learned was

the process counts.

A Match Made in Heaven

Jesus walks a "marriage" process too. In ancient Israel, there were steps toward marriage, steps that Jesus willingly and patiently took, and is still taking, so that He can appropriately lay the foundation for a relationship and a future with us.

He doesn't have to do it. He is the King of kings and Lord of lords; He's the One who makes the rules. Amazingly, though, once He sets a rule in place, He follows it too. We have an example in Scripture. When John the Baptist protested about baptizing Jesus, Jesus replied, "Permit it to be so now, for thus it is fitting for us to fulfill all righteousness."[3]

In essence, He was saying, "There's a right way and a wrong way to do it, John. And even though this step seems unnecessary, let's do it anyway. Let's do it the right way."

Jesus cares about the process; and in order to "do it right," He's willing to wait for us, just as He calls us to wait for Him.

The ancient Hebrew betrothal process began with the selection of the bride, and it was not uncommon for the father of the potential groom to make those arrangements. We see an example of this in the life of Abraham, when he sent his servant to find a bride for Isaac.

Now Jesus whispers His words of selection to us, His Beloved:

You did not choose Me, but I chose you.[4]

I have redeemed you; I have called you by your name;
You are Mine.[5]

When the final agreement was established, the bridegroom and bride met—sometimes for the first time—with their fathers. The bridegroom was expected to bring:

- the bride price (though paid to the bride's family, this was intended to belong to the bride herself),
- the *ketubah* (the contract in which was written the promises and terms of the marriage), and
- a gift for the bride.

Scripture tells us that we're "the church of God which He purchased with His own blood."[6] Jesus gave everything so that He could win us! The apostle Paul passionately writes:

Do you not know that your body
is the temple of the Holy Spirit who is in you,
whom you have from God, and you are not your own?
For you were bought at a price.[7]

I once heard a rabbi say that the *ketubah*—the betrothal contract—from God to Israel was established at Mount Sinai with the
giving of the Law. But now in Jesus, our *ketubah*—our promise, our
covenant—is not written on stone, but on our hearts. Jesus comes
with a *ketubah* of passion and with a bride price purchased with His
own blood.

You are an epistle of Christ . . .
written not with ink but by the Spirit of the living God,
not on tablets of stone but on tablets of flesh, that is, of the heart.[8]

I will give you a new heart and put a new spirit within you;
I will take the heart of stone out of your flesh
and give you a heart of flesh.[9]

When these gifts were accepted, the drinking of wine together
sealed the betrothal. The couple was now considered married, though
the wedding was yet in the future—as long as two years away. We see
Jesus movingly seal our betrothal on the night before His death:

Then He took the cup, and gave thanks,
and gave it to them, saying,
"Drink from it, all of you.
For this is My blood of the new covenant,
which is shed for many for the remission of sins . . .
I will not drink of this fruit of the vine from now on until
that day when I drink it new with you
in My Father's kingdom."[10]

During the time between the betrothal and the wedding, the
bride and the groom each had responsibilities. The groom, in particular, was to prepare a place for his bride. The father of the groom was
the one who determined when the *chuppah* (or marriage canopy) was

fully ready. He is the one who decided when the last nail had been pounded in, the last detail attended to, and the last curtain hung. The father inspected all, and only when he approved it was the bridegroom released to go to receive his bride.

The word *chuppah* is used only three times in the Old Testament.[11] Twice it describes its typical use for a wedding. But the third time, in Isaiah 4:5, the prophet uses it to describe the fact that God wants to dwell with all of His people. It says, "then the Lord will create above every dwelling place of Mount Zion, and above her assemblies, a cloud and smoke by day and the shining of a flaming fire by night. For over all the glory there will be a *chuppah*."

Upon every dwelling place.

That's where *you* live. That's where *I* live.

There's no other way to interpret "every" except that God is offering this to everyone! *Upon every dwelling place . . . His glory will be a chuppah*—a marriage canopy, where He can meet and dwell and have intimate relationship with us.

The bride had responsibilities during this time as well. Following the betrothal, she began to prepare for her marriage. Presumably she was excused from some of her other responsibilities so that she could devote her time to getting ready. She prepared the household goods that she would need and, of course, her wedding garment. In fact, part of her "job" was to look beautiful at all times because she didn't know when her beloved would come for her. "Being ready" was a primary responsibility.

She was considered to be *set apart*; in Hebrew, literally, *sanctify*.[12] Don't let that word scare you. We sometimes overthink sanctification, but, simply put, it means to purify. Which was another part of the bride's process—the *mikvah*—immersing herself in water for cleansing and purification. Washing in water. It was literally a baptism.

Set apart.

Baptized.

Ready at all times.

Does this sound vaguely familiar to you? It should! It's our process too. Paul writes:

> *I have betrothed you to one husband,*
> *that I may present you as a chaste virgin to Christ.*[13]

We're prepared to meet Him, and He is preparing the chamber.[14] Jesus said that only the Father knows the day or the hour,[15] because it is the Father who has to approve the marriage canopy. Then Jesus will come . . .

> *like a bridegroom coming out of his [chuppah],*
> *[rejoicing] like a strong man to run its race.*[16]

This verse has often been viewed as describing a young man leaving his marriage bed, happy and fulfilled.

But I beg to differ.

First of all, there is no mention of the bride. Second, have you ever seen a man on his honeymoon leave his bride behind? I don't think so. All you need is a trip to Hawaii to see that honeymooning couples stick pretty close together. No—this is a bridegroom whose father has just "approved the *chuppah*," and he is now racing to his bride.

Once the father gave his approval, the bridegroom was released to go get his bride and bring her back to the place he had prepared. This was done with fanfare and surprise—sometimes in the middle of the night, "like a thief," at an unexpected moment. Part of the fun and expectancy was to be prepared at *all times* so that whenever the bridegroom came, he would find his beloved ready and waiting for him. At this time, the marriage would take place and the marriage supper celebrated.

> *For the Lord Himself will descend from heaven with a shout,*
> *with the voice of an archangel, and with the trumpet of God.*[17]

> *For you yourselves know perfectly that*
> *the day of the Lord so comes as a thief in the night.*[18]

> *Behold, I am coming as a thief.*
> *Blessed is he who watches, and keeps his garments.*[19]

It isn't difficult to see Jesus' faithfulness to the process. Right now, He is preparing to receive us, and we are to be preparing to go to Him

in purity,

in watchfulness,

in expectancy,

in love.

The Rules of Engagement

During my children's engagements, I learned that there is a lot going on during any couple's preparation for marriage. The couple is transitioning into a new commitment, making decisions and learning how to communicate. They are determining the details of their new life together, determining financial matters and merging schedules.

That's a lot to think about!

I've watched brides collect family recipes, start looking at decorating magazines and ask numerous household management questions. Grooms start asking about insurance, investments and rent. And they suddenly converse comfortably about paint colors, pots and pans and, yes—he really *does* want a quesadilla maker.

As soon as "the question is popped," a relationship completely shifts gears. One of our brides leapt into action the day following her engagement. Wedding plans were definitely in full swing. The poor groom-to-be felt a little bewildered with the To Do lists that were suddenly coming his way. In conversation one day, I laughingly asked him if he wondered what happened to his girlfriend.

As the words came out of my mouth, however, I realized that what had happened was that she wasn't a girlfriend any longer—she was becoming a wife. Commitment had changed the focus of their relationship, and they were entering a new stage of learning about each other; they were taking the beginning steps of

building a solid foundation.

Jesus talked about this.[20] He described two builders. One took the time to dig down to bedrock and establish his house on a foundation that was unshakable and unassailable by the elements.

The other wanted the quick answer and the beachfront property, so he built his house on the sand.

The storms of life invariably assaulted both of these men's homes. One building withstood the storm; the other did not. Ultimately, the biggest "why" of walking the process in a relationship—whether it's with a person or with Jesus—is that it takes time to build something permanent.

As the Bride of Christ, we are learning to live in an entirely new Kingdom! And living in that Kingdom is supposed to impact everything.

As surely as I started to change the way I did things when I moved toward marriage—learning some of Scott's mom's recipes, choosing items for our home, and shifting my focus forward—our life in Jesus is supposed to reflect that we now belong to the One who is part of the largest and smallest decisions of life. We are being called to talk differently, pursue different interests and banish compromise from our lives. We're called to obey Him, put our finances under His control and accept the disciplines of living for Him.

It's also a time of learning our rights and privileges as the Bride of the King of kings. Casting shame and blame aside, He calls us to minister in His name, accept His Holy Spirit-inspired gifts, stand as royalty, and bring His message and love to the world around us.

We're in an engagement period with Jesus, and the foundation of our future is being laid—here and now.

---

1. See Revelation 21:10,14.
2. Deuteronomy 6:7-9.
3. Matthew 3:15.
4. John 15:16.
5. Isaiah 43:1.
6. Acts 20:28.
7. 1 Corinthians 6:19-20.
8. 2 Corinthians 3:3.
9. Ezekiel 36:26.
10. Matthew 26:27-29.
11. See Psalm 19:5, Isaiah 4:5, Joel 2:16.
12. James Strong, The New Strong's Exhaustive Concordance of the Bible (Nashville, TN: Thomas Nelson, 1995), Hebrew #6942.
13. 2 Corinthians 11:2.
14. See John 14:2-3.
15. See Mark 13:32.
16. Psalm 19:5.
17. 1 Thessalonians 4:16.
18. 1 Thessalonians 5:2.
19. Revelation 16:15.
20. See Matthew 7:24-29.

Encountering Him

FIRST THINGS FIRST

Psalm 22:3 says that the Lord is enthroned on the praises of His people. Think about what that means: Every time we give ourselves in praise to Him, we are also building a throne for Him to rule in our lives, and inviting His presence wherever we are. It's part of the process of "learning to live with Him." We're building a foundation.

That verse doesn't present an isolated concept.

When the Tabernacle was set up, God's presence was manifested following Moses' faithfulness to build "according to the pattern." At the dedication of Solomon's Temple, God's presence entered following extravagant sacrifice and worship.[1] Further, the psalmist calls us to "enter into His gates with thanksgiving, and into His courts with praise."[2] And, given the fact that several places in Scripture call our mouths "doors,"[3] a significant parallel is presented when we read:

> *Lift up your heads, O you gates! . . .*
> *And the King of glory shall come in.*[4]

In my walk with the Lord, I have found this to be true: One of the surest ways to invite the Lord's presence is through worship. In this encounter, I'm inviting you to do the same. If we are going to walk with Jesus as our Bridegroom, then inviting His presence is the most basic part of our process.

I've compiled a list of worship songs, coordinated with the chapter themes. Some of these are new songs; some are older. I'm sure you have your favorites too, but this will give you a start. All of the music is available on iTunes; and I would encourage you as you go through this book to regularly spend time in worship—inviting the Lord's presence into your home, your car, your office and your life.

1. Love Letters
   "How Great Is the Love"—Paul Baloche, *Glorious*
   "Jesus, Lover of My Soul"—Darlene Zschech, *Worship Celebration*

2. **First Comes Love**
   "The Beauty of the Bride"—Steve Green, *Where Mercy Begins*
   "Here I Am to Worship"—Tim Hughes, *Here I Am to Worship*

3. **Meet Him Again**
   "Amazed"—Lincoln Brewster, *All to You . . . Live*
   "Holy Spirit Rain Down"—World's Best Praise and Worship,
   Days of Elijah

4. **The Passion**
   "We Will Remember"—Tommy Walker, *Break Through*
   "Beautiful One"—Tim Hughes, *When Silence Falls*

5. **The Choice**
   "Trading My Sorrows"—Darrell Evans, *Trading My Sorrows—
   The Best of Darrell Evans*
   "Blessed Be the Name of the Lord"—Matt Redman,
   Blessed Be the Name of the Lord

6. **The Proposal**
   "Breathe"—Michael W. Smith, *Worship*
   "You Are the One"—Lincoln Brewster, *All to You . . . Live*

7. **The Diamond**
   "You Are My All in All"—Bob Fitts, *He Will Save You (Live)*
   "Worthy Is the Lamb"—Brooklyn Tabernacle Choir,
   I'll Say Yes (Live)

8. **The Gown**
   "You Are Holy"—Christ for the Nations Music, *Perfect Love
   (Live)*
   "Here in Your Presence"—New Life Worship, *My Savior Lives*

9. **The Name**
   "He Knows My Name"—Tommy Walker, *Alone with God . . .
   I Will Be with You*
   "Name Above All Names"—Chuck Girard, *Name Above
   All Names*

10. **The Partnership**
    "Pour My Love on You"—Craig and Dean Phillips, *Let My Words Be Few*
    "Broken and Spilled Out"—Steve Green, *The Ultimate Collection*

11. **Love Triumphant**
    "You Gave Your Life Away"—Paul Baloche, *Our God Saves*
    "At the Cross"—Hillsong Live, *Mighty to Save (Live)*

12. **He's Worth the Wait**
    "This Could Be the Day"—Steve Amerson, *This Could Be the Day*
    "Days of Elijah"—World's Best Praise and Worship, *Days of Elijah*

---

1. See Exodus 40; 1 Kings 8.
2. Psalm 100:4.
3. See Psalm 141:3; Micah 7:5.
4. Psalm 24:9.

MEET HIM AGAIN

I remember the very first time I saw James. He and Lindsey were walking together after a youth group event. I had never seen him before, but what stood out to me was the light in both of their eyes as they talked. Sparks were flying everywhere.

Who is that guy? I wondered.

I discovered later that they had only met that day, but the interest was clearly there from the start. However, a solid relational foundation isn't built on sparks.

They needed time—time for Lindsey to get out of high school (James was a college freshman), and time to find out if this was even capable of growing into anything, which is what friendships are for.

They were simply getting to know each other. They saw each other in youth group, at youth events and at ministry outreaches. They talked a lot. They discovered they had shared interests, a similar sense of humor, and an identical focus for their lives. They were headed in the same direction. They both felt called to ministry and, in fact, she was already planning to go to the same Bible college he was enrolled in. They learned a lot about each other while they were still "just friends."

They started dating about a year later, but I was there when it all started!

Brian and Melissa were an entirely different story. They had actually met in a play when they were in elementary school, but then Melissa's family changed churches. Their paths didn't cross again until they were in high school. Melissa wasn't in the same grade as any of our children, so I only knew her from a distance. But I remember the first conversation I had with her.

She was working at Maloney's Stationery Store, and our family had walked in after having dinner at the restaurant next door. I needed to pick up a couple of birthday cards.

Suddenly, a young woman dashed across the store and ran up to Brian. (Parents notice these things!) As it turned out, they were on student council together, and she came over just to say hello. Scott talked to her. Brian and Kyle parked themselves in the aisle with the Far Side cards. And because she worked in the store, she helped me find what I needed.

I never forgot that first meeting with her, though it would be years before there was any romantic connection between her and Brian.

Though they had met before, they needed a chance to meet again.

Meeting Jesus Again

Sometimes we need a chance to meet Jesus again too. I'm not talking about salvation; I'm talking about our preconceived notions of Him. Sometimes we walk with Him so long that we "get used" to Him and wind up making assumptions about Him that aren't true.

For example, I once declined eating blueberries at a friend's house. The next time I was there, she said, "Oh, I know you hate blueberries." Actually, I don't mind blueberries; I just hadn't wanted them that one day. But based on one response, she made an assumption about me that wasn't true.

We do the same thing with Jesus—and, now, it's time to meet Him again.

Though they had met before,
they needed a chance to meet again.

The need to "meet Jesus again" isn't something new. It happened to two people in the Bible—Jesus' mother, and His best friend.

I've always been impressed with Mary. She had miraculous encounters unlike anyone before or after her. She gave birth to the Son of God. She encountered angels. She saw miracles. She witnessed the Resurrection.

She and Joseph also ran for their lives from Herod. She was separated from her family during the "Egypt years." And she watched her son die a gruesome death on a Roman cross.

Yes, she had quite a life, and she knew Jesus like no one else.

She heard His first words and helped Him learn how to walk. She packed His lunch for a day in the carpentry shop with Joseph. She held His hand at the market. She celebrated the festivals with Him and saw His face in awe the first time He saw the temple in Jerusalem. She taught Him prayers, told Him stories and made Him treats.

If there was anyone who has ever earned the right to say "been there, done that" when it came to a relationship with Jesus, it was Mary. Yet the last mention of her in Scripture is in the book of Acts. After Jesus' resurrection, and after the ascension, she was with the disciples in the Upper Room, waiting for the next thing that God wanted to do. And Mary became part of the church of Jesus Christ on the day of Pentecost!

Amazing woman. Amazing humility. She was willing to "meet Jesus again"—not simply as her son, but as her Savior and Lord.

Another person who met Jesus "again" was John. He knew Jesus and knew Him well. As one of Jesus' disciples, he had walked countless miles and sat around a thousand fires, sharing meals with Jesus and the other disciples. John was also one of Jesus' inner circle. Beyond being Jesus' disciple, they were also friends. John knew Jesus' heart. His humor. His compassion. "The disciple Jesus loved," Scripture calls him.

So what would you do if suddenly, like John, Jesus showed up looking different than you remembered Him? And what would it mean for your friendship to have Him so changed? What if your best friend showed up one day as a *king*? John describes his experience:

I was in the Spirit on the Lord's Day, and I heard behind me a loud voice, as of a trumpet, saying, "I am the Alpha and the Omega, the First and the Last" . . . Then I turned to see the voice that spoke with me. And having turned I saw seven golden lampstands, and in the midst of the seven lampstands One like the Son of Man, clothed with a garment down to the feet and girded about the chest with a golden band. His head and hair were white like wool, as white as snow, and His eyes like a flame of fire; His feet were like fine brass, as if refined in a furnace, and His voice as the sound of many waters; He had in His right hand seven stars, out of His mouth went a sharp two-edged sword, and His countenance was like the sun shining in its strength. And when I saw Him, I fell at His feet as dead. But He laid His right hand on me, saying to me, "Do not be afraid; I am the First and the Last. I am He who lives, and was dead, and behold, I am alive forevermore. Amen. And I have the keys of Hades and of Death."[1]

Jesus is, in effect, reintroducing Himself to John.

And He's reintroducing Himself to us too.

The description is stunning. The only other time Jesus would have looked anything like this would have been at His transfiguration, when Scripture says that His garments were as white as the light.[2] But now . . . *now* . . .

> girded with gold
> > white as snow
> > > eyes like fire
> > > > voice like a torrent

No wonder John fell at His feet as though dead.

In the following chapter, as John begins to write to each of the churches, parts of this description are used to introduce Jesus in each letter. As with other parts of the letters, I grew up only hearing them presented negatively. For example, "His feet are like fine brass" was taught to me almost as if Jesus were charging through my life stomping out everything of unworthiness in me. "He has a sharp two-edged sword" was communicated to me that now Jesus was stomping *and* swinging a sword. It was scary! If that's what Jesus was like, I wasn't sure I wanted to meet Him in person. *"Knowing You from a distance is fine with me, Lord. Thank You very much."*

I needed to meet Him again.

I have no intention of making light of how Jesus deals with us. Does He ever confront us with that kind of intensity? The answer is, yes, He does. But to interpret His introduction as *only* that loses other things that Jesus wanted to communicate to His Church, His beloved, His Bride. When He invited John—and the churches, and us—to meet Him again, He was showing more than confrontation. He was showing

> majesty
> > passion
> > > beauty
> > > > royalty
> > > > > glory

He's everything you would ever hope a Bridegroom would be.

The Man of Your Dreams

Maybe you, like I, need to take another look at how Jesus introduced Himself, to see the heart of love behind it. These were never intended to be words of fear. Inherent in each introduction is hope, truth, love and faithfulness. As we look at themes in the introductions to the letters, we see Jesus

> ignite passion
>> confront with compassion
>>> protect the future
>>>> complete His work

The Igniter—Tending Passion's Flame

In two of the letters, Jesus introduces Himself as the One who has "the seven stars," "seven lampstands" and "the seven spirits of God." The symbolism of the stars and lampstands has already been identified for us:

> *The seven stars are the angels of the seven churches,*
> *and the seven lampstands which you saw are the seven churches.*[3]

Though it is not specifically mentioned that the lampstands had flames burning, it would most definitely have been the case. Jesus said, "No one, when he has lit a lamp, puts it in a secret place or under a basket, but on a lampstand, that those who come in may see the light."[4] We should expect no less when it comes to His Church. Further, in His final hours, Jesus promises His disciples that He will send His Spirit[5]—a promise fulfilled with flames of fire on the day of Pentecost. The Church is intended to carry the flame of His Spirit.

Now, Jesus walks among the churches, not only as the igniter of the flame, but as the One who tends it. He is examining each church, seeing where a flame needs to be refueled, finding out why a flame is burning low, trimming a wick so that the flame burns bright again. Isaiah wrote, "A smoking wick He will not put out."[6] This isn't judgment. It's love. It's the Lover of our souls tending the passion in our hearts and seeking to see that it stays ignited and burning bright.

Jesus warns the church at Ephesus to repent "or else I will come to you quickly and remove your lampstand."[7] The word "quickly" is the same word used later for His return.[8]

He is not saying that He's giving them five minutes to shape up or He is going to crush their lamp out. This isn't Jesus delightedly rubbing His hands together, hoping He can call down judgment on the Church. Jesus takes no pleasure in destroying people. When His disciples suggested calling down fire to consume people, He answered, "You do not know what manner of spirit you are of. For the Son of Man did not come to destroy men's lives but to save them."[9]

This is Jesus with tears in His eyes and longing in His voice, calling His Beloved back to the fire of passion she once had. His intent, as with a loving Bridegroom, is to give time as long as there is hope that the Beloved will respond and turn back to Him with passion and love and commitment. He longs

>to woo her
>>to win her again
>>>to bring love back to what it once was
>>>>to re-ignite passion

The prophet Zechariah saw the lampstand too. He wrote, "I am looking, and there is a lampstand of solid gold with a bowl on top of it, and on the stand seven lamps."[10] The temptation—as it was with the churches in Revelation and with us—is to try to re-ignite passion on our own. And Zechariah urged the people of his day, as Jesus urges us now: It's " 'Not by might nor by power, but by My Spirit,' says the LORD of hosts."[11] The flame of passion cannot be sustained by our own efforts. It is only through the continued grace and gift of Jesus' Spirit in us.

The Confronter—Compassion's Work

We can get so caught up in the romance of God's love for us that we leave unacknowledged the fact that true love will also inspire growth. When we come to the Lord, we come to the One who knows all hearts. He looks beyond mere actions—He knows what your intent is; He knows where your heart is broken; He knows why you are trying to protect yourself.

And He will grow you beyond that.

I already mentioned my experiences as a young girl in hearing that Jesus was a warrior with fire in His eyes and a sword in His hand. I never want to belittle or ignore the fact that Jesus *does* come to challenge us to growth. He wants to move us out of our comfort zone and reveal our hearts. But what was overlooked in how I was taught was that when He comes to confront, He comes with endless compassion. He is here to challenge and confront, not crush and intimidate.

We see His compassion in John's description of Jesus' feet being made of fine brass. Throughout Scripture, "brass" is used to represent suffering and sacrifice. For example, the altar in the Tabernacle—the place of sacrifice—was made of brass.

Jesus' feet of brass are to remind us that He has walked the road of humanity. He came and offered Himself in our place. He was our sacrifice; He took our suffering. Yes, He has a sword. But His sword divides soul and spirit, joints and marrow, thoughts and intents.[12] He is compassionate and lovingly relentless in freeing us from the things that hold us back from realizing all He has for us.

One of Scott's lifelong objectives with me was to challenge my tendency to negativity. When we were engaged, I asked him once to tell me what needed correcting in me. I have no idea, now, what led to the question, but the love letter that follows is part of his much lengthier response. If you will, consider that if an earthly husband would be so careful and kind in confronting, why do we think that Jesus, in all of His perfection, would be any different?

Love Letter

How can I tell of your faults when I only think of your goodness? How can I speak of your weaknesses when I derive so much strength knowing that you are with me? How can I tell you what's wrong when I love you so much?

Alas, though my heart be wrenched in two to even consider that you may not be perfect, I will tell you since it is the desire of the heart of my lady fair. You have asked me what be your greatest shortcomings (oh, the pain of consideration).

My dear, it appears at times to me that your lips doth criticize what your eyes doth see.

sgb to rlb, 1976

Compassion? Yes. Challenging me to grow? Yes. A good husband is like that, because he saw the potential in me and wanted me to be everything I could be.

Just like Jesus.

The Protector—Open Doors, Closed Doors

As surely as Jesus challenges and confronts, He also protects. One of the ways He protects is seen in how He introduces Himself in the letter to Philadelphia. Jesus is the one "who has the key of David, He who opens and no one shuts, and shuts and no one opens."[13] Here we see doors of potential and doors of protection.

As New Testament believers, we tend to think of God in terms of open doors. There is forward motion in our lives, and we have a greater sense of His purpose in and through us. Open doors are exciting!

New opportunities. New ministry. New adventure.

We will talk more about open doors in a moment, but Scripture also has a surprising amount to say about "closed doors." We don't like to talk about those. Yet there isn't any one of us that would not look back and honestly admit that there have been doors in our lives that God has closed.

And it became a protection to us.

Closed doors can be as positive and as filled with possibility as open doors can be.

There is the door of salvation. While coming to Jesus opens "life and life more abundant," it also closes the door on a past that we no longer pursue. That is a significant and sometimes difficult decision to make.

The account of the first Passover—a powerful prefiguring of the cross—illustrates the door of salvation.[14] The children of Israel were called to sacrifice the Passover lamb and put the blood on the doorposts of their homes. They were then instructed, "None of you shall go out of the door until the morning."

They were behind closed doors, and what was provided through obedience to those instructions literally was salvation and life. The blood of the lamb was upon those doorposts, and the people inside

Be strong and of good courage . . . for the LORD your God, He is the One
who goes with you. He will not leave you nor forsake you.[25]

And I will pray the Father, and He will give you another Helper,
that He may abide with you forever.[26]

In many respects, the book of Revelation ends the same as it began:
Jesus restates His names
He extends His promise
His focus is again on His Bride—the Church—
and He calls, "I'm coming quickly!
Be ready for the wedding!"[27]

The letters to the churches are nothing to fear, but they do call us
to response—response to the One who promises to stay, who promises
to complete, who promises to love
forever.

He was supreme in the beginning and—leading the resurrection parade—
he is supreme in the end. From beginning to end he's there,
towering far above everything, everyone.[28]

---

1. Revelation 1:10-18.
2. See Matthew 17:2.
3. Revelation 1:20.
4. Luke 11:33.
5. See John 15:26.
6. Isaiah 42:3, author's paraphrase.
7. Revelation 2:5.
8. See Revelation 22:20.
9. Luke 9:55-56.
10. Zechariah 4:2.
11. Zechariah 4:6.
12. See Hebrews 4:12.
13. Revelation 3:7.
14. See Exodus 12.
15. See Exodus 12:38.
16. Genesis 7:16.
17. See 2 Kings 4:4.
18. See Matthew 6:6.
19. See Matthew 25:10.
20. See Acts 14:27.
21. See Acts 16:26.
22. See 1 Corinthians 16:9.
23. Matthew 28:1-2.
24. John 10:9.
25. Deuteronomy 31:6.
26. John 14:16.
27. See Revelation 22.
28. Colossians 1:18, *THE MESSAGE*.

Encountering Him

THE BRIDE PRICE

We've been talking about meeting Jesus "again," but perhaps you have never met Him for the first time. If you have never asked Jesus Christ to be your Savior, it's as simple as looking and finding Him. The Bible says, "And you will seek Me and find Me, when you search for Me with all your heart."[1]

Jesus is looking and finding too. We read that "the Son of Man has come to seek and to save that which was lost."[2]

Being lost includes all of us. We were lost in darkness, caught by sin and living in disobedience. But Jesus came to find us! It is Jesus, Himself, who said:

> *God so loved the world that He gave His only begotten Son,*
> *that whoever believes in Him should not perish*
> *but have everlasting life. For God did not send His Son into*
> *the world to condemn the world,*
> *but that the world through Him might be saved.*[3]

The Bible also tells us that:

> *If you confess with your mouth the Lord Jesus and believe in your*
> *heart that God has raised Him from the dead, you will be saved.*[4]

If you've never met Jesus for the first time, may I invite you to pray these words:

Dear Father God,
I come to You in the name of Your Son, Jesus, who died for me. I thank You that You love me, and I ask that, as Your Word promises, You would come to me as I have sought You.

Thank You for the gift of Your Son. Thank You for the fact that He has suffered and sacrificed for me and has taken the punishment I deserved. I lay my life before You and ask that You forgive me for every instance I have sinned, every place that I have fallen short of what You desire for my life. I lay all of my sin, guilt, shame and incompleteness before You. I am sorry for all that I have done wrong.

I ask You to forgive me, to fill my life and to make me complete. I ask You to cleanse me from all sin by the blood and sacrifice of Jesus. Thank You that now I am forgiven and have accepted the "life and life more abundant" that is Your promise to Your children.

Now, I give my life to Jesus Christ, the Son of God. I turn from my way to Your way. I ask that You walk with me through all of my life. I ask that Your Holy Spirit fill me and direct me into new life with You.

In the name of Jesus Christ, our risen Savior and Lord. Amen.

Or You May Need to Meet Jesus Again . . .

You may have known the Lord for decades, but now you need to "meet Him again." You may have preconceived ideas about Him, as we talked about earlier. Or you may have found that your relationship simply has grown stale.

Jesus has more for you.

When He came, He came to offer salvation for our souls, healing for our bodies, freedom for our hearts. Whatever you have experienced of Jesus so far, He has more for you.

I've often wondered how people view salvation. Some treat it as though it were only an "eternal issue," and they can go on living however they did before they met Him. But salvation is intended to extend into all of life, now and forever.

Still, there are some who treat salvation as though a lifeguard saved them from drowning and then just left them lying on the beach. Soaked. Cold. Barely breathing. Yes, their life was saved, but there is little else going for them.

Can I say it again? *Jesus has more for you!* So, may I invite you to meet Him again? Not for salvation . . . that's been done. But for everything else He promises:

> *I have come that they may have life,*
> *and that they may have it more abundantly.*[5]
>
> *Ask, and you will receive, that your joy may be full.*[6]

Peace I leave with you, My peace I give to you;
not as the world gives do I give to you.
Let not your heart be troubled, neither let it be afraid.[7]

Would you join me in this prayer:

Dear Heavenly Father,
I come before You today to ask that You help me to see Jesus freshly. I want to meet Him again.

• *I don't want to come in my fear of condemnation—I know that isn't from You.*
• *I want to be rid of my preconceived ideas of what I think about You— You're so much bigger than what I can ever imagine!*
• *And I don't want to be a child who misrepresents You—I want to live as though You've done the most for me, not the least for me.*
• *I want to receive from Your hand everything You offer to me.*

I lay all of these attitudes at Your feet and ask that You open my eyes to see You in a brand-new way. I want to meet You again, see Your heart and hear Your voice.
I ask this in the name of Jesus. Amen.

---

1. Jeremiah 29:13.
2. Luke 19:10.
3. John 3:16-17.
4. Romans 10:9.
5. John 10:10.
6. John 16:24.
7. John 14:27.

THE 7 LOVE LETTERS FROM Jesus

THE PASSION

When Scott and I first met, we were both in college, both working full time and both as broke as could be. Seriously . . . all of our money went to school, so a "big date" was Bob's Big Boy restaurant, aka "Robert's at the Mall"—our euphemism to make it sound nicer than it actually was! Nothing against Bob's Big Boy, but it isn't usually the first place you think of for dinner when you're considering a romantic evening out!

Our courtship was wonderful anyway. It didn't matter that dates were at Bob's Big Boy, or McDonald's. It didn't matter that Scott picked flowers for me out of the backyard or off of the fence at work. Actually, a lot of our time was spent at our parents' homes, at church and on the phone. Being together was worth more than a fancy surrounding. Getting to know each other was exciting and filled with joy. And every touch of his hand made me tingle all over!

Sigh. It was lovely!

It was so wonderful that we decided we wanted to spend the rest of our lives together! So Scott offered—and I accepted—a lovely proposal, a gorgeous diamond and beautiful flowers. After that, we started planning our version of a "white lace and promises" wedding. Followed by a romantic honeymoon. Lots of presents. Setting up our first home.

Even lovelier! And then . . .

I suddenly added to my full-time-student-full-time-job schedule the responsibilities of a home. Now I had to cook three meals a day (Mom's cooking never sounded so good!) and do the laundry (except without an in-house washer and dryer . . . pass the quarters, please), and do the grocery shopping (we knew every 24-hour market in our area because sometimes the only time we were able to shop was at midnight), and pay the bills (more of *those* than I'd ever had before!), and clean the house (that apartment was getting bigger and dirtier by the minute). While we were basking in the glow of beginning our new life, dust was still accumulating and the grass was still growing. Let's get real . . . passion doesn't get the work done!

My head was spinning with responsibility. I was 19, and married, and trying to figure out how to juggle it all. I mean, the leap from "flowers and candy" to "flour and canned goods" is a big one.

Yes, that leap began with passion. There's no denying that.

But passion was never intended to stand alone. Passion has a purpose. Passion is meant to *lead* you somewhere. Our world, it seems, has largely forgotten this and pursues passion for its own sake. Our wise Creator, however, intended passion to flow into covenant and commitment—a promise to love, to commit our lives to one another, and to build a future together.

Passion brought Scott and me to a point of choosing covenant, but "the promise" also brought with it responsibility. Think about that a minute—all of that responsibility landed in our laps *because passion had entered our lives.*

Suddenly we weren't just "looking at blueprints" anymore; we were building. We were no longer planning, talking and preparing; we were *doing.*

> Passion
> Covenant
> Responsibility

Each is the natural outflow of the other, but they are intended to be cumulative. Ultimately, passion and responsibility, based in covenant, are supposed to go hand in hand. The challenge isn't in the doing but in forgetting *why* you're doing *what* you're doing.

Responsibility came because passion had entered our lives.

....

I watched that "leap" again about 25 years later, when RESPONSIBILITY hit as each of my children got engaged. From a mother's point of view, however, I usually saw it hit the groom first.

The poor young groom! He is suddenly trying to figure out how he is going to deal with the cost of living. Never mind the old saying, two do *not* eat as cheaply as one. The groom is looking for an apartment, checking out electricity costs and trying to get his car paid off before the wedding. He wants to bump up his savings, find insurance policies and figure out a budget. Of course, he also has to plan—and pay for—the honeymoon.

My son Kyle recalls looking at his salary and wondering if they could live on one salary if Teresa got pregnant on the honeymoon. He felt like he had to have a back-up plan if the unexpected happened. "Because," he said, "once you're having sex, the unexpected becomes a possibility!" He also felt the need to identify and define goals for the future—God-given call, purpose and mission. What are our "next steps" supposed to be? What are we aiming at? How do we begin *building a life*?

On the other hand, the bride gets to plan the wedding. Upon her engagement, one of my daughters-in-law-to-be put together a wedding notebook. In it was everything she had to do, and it ran her life for the next eight months. It had checklists, appointments, countdowns and schedules. Fabric samples, pictures, ideas and phone numbers. Addresses, caterers and, well, you get the idea. Lots of fun!

My son called that notebook "The Beast."

....

When my daughter got engaged, she was given the wedding-fund money that we had saved. I told her that I didn't care how she spent the money. It had been saved for her, and this was her wedding. She could do as she pleased (except elope to Las Vegas and pocket the funds). My only maxim was "I'm committed to the budget." My son-in-law-to-be took this very seriously and presented me with a weekly spreadsheet on how the money was being spent.

This wedding thing is serious business!

Because responsibility flows from passion.

....

When Jesus wrote to the church at Ephesus, He was dealing with a similar issue. The Ephesians were a hard-working bunch. Responsibility had flowed out of passion. But at some point (and probably no one could identify when or where) they crossed the line of doing for doing's sake. "Keep on keepin' on" could have been their slogan. They were *doing* everything right.

But they had somehow misplaced the passion that had started it all.

To the angel of the church of Ephesus write, "These things says He who holds the seven stars in His right hand, who walks in the midst of the seven golden lampstands. 'I know your works, your labor, your patience, and that you cannot bear those who are evil. And you have tested those who say they are apostles and are not, and have found them liars; and you have persevered and have patience, and have labored for My name's sake and have not become weary. Nevertheless I have this against you, that you have left your first love. Remember therefore from where you have fallen; repent and do the first works, or else I will come to you quickly and remove your lampstand from its place—unless you repent. But this you have, that you hate the deeds of the Nicolaitans, which I also hate. He who has an ear, let him hear what the Spirit says to the churches. To him who overcomes I will give to eat from the tree of life, which is in the midst of the Paradise of God.' "[1]

The subheading in my Bible for this letter is: "The Loveless Church."[2] I have to admit that I chuckled to myself when I read that title. How like we humans to leap to the worst possible interpretation. Yet, "loveless church" isn't what Jesus said. He didn't say they were "loveless." He said:

You have left your first love.

He also said that He knows how hard they have worked for Him.

Works. Labor. Patience. Discernment. Perseverance.

Those characteristics are all noted—and commended—as being a part of the life of this church. As believers, we look at these attributes in a very positive way. And they're all good traits for us to have. They are a sign of maturity, diligence, faithfulness, and responsibility.

But God looks at the heart.[3]

Our Bridegroom looks at the motive behind what we're doing. He wants to know that what we are *doing* is because we love Him, and not because we "have to" or we're "supposed to" or we "owe it to Him." All of us are tempted to default to simply doing tasks rather than investing in a relationship. Tasks are easy to check off of the To Do list. Nurturing passion in relationships is trickier.

Do you remember when you first encountered Jesus? You couldn't stop talking about Him. Reading the Word was a delight. Prayer and worship seemed to constantly flow from your innermost being. "First love" looks like that! First love is wonderful. First love blinds you to imperfections. And in the case of our Bridegroom, He has no imperfections. We can look at Jesus and truly say, "He is perfect! He is the greatest. He can take care of anything." He can probably even fix the plumbing—after all, He was raised by a carpenter.

First Love. Passion.

You accepted Jesus' offer of love—salvation. And in love, you began to attend church, teach a Sunday School class, sing in the choir, go to Bible study, help clean the sanctuary, decorate for the Christmas service, clean up after a church dinner. *Whew!* Before you knew it, your calendar was packed and all you could do was run to keep up. Your neighbors didn't know your name, but they saw you constantly pulling out of the driveway. They wondered why you were so busy, because you didn't seem particularly happy. But . . . you'd checked everything off of your To Do list.

Somewhere in the process, however, you looked up and it seemed like Jesus was so far, far away. *How did that happen?*

The truth is that passion may inspire responsibility, but whether we like it or not, all of our action—all of our doing—is rarely going to inspire passion. How often, like the Ephesians, we get busy for the Lord and forget our first love. In nurturing our relationship with Jesus, I don't know that the things we're *doing* necessarily change, but they come from our heart and not only our hand.

I have had seasons in my life when I read my Bible reading "quota" for the day so that it could be done and checked off. Obviously, that checkmark, gratifying as it might feel, was never the point. Developing the habit was good. Reading the Word was good, even commendable. But the Spirit of the Word didn't penetrate very deeply that day. Nurturing my relationship with the Lord requires that when I read my Bible, I come to it with a heart open to hear His voice, not just quickly read words.

That's just one example, of course, from one area of life. Even so, I never want to be a person who *does* all of the right things but hasn't developed the relationship that matters. Jesus said that in the end times, there will be people like that—people who have done all of the correct actions but simply do not know Him. Terrible thought!

> *Many will say to Me in that day, "Lord, Lord, have we not prophesied in Your name, cast out demons in Your name, and done many wonders in Your name?" And then I will declare to them, "I never knew you."*[4]

Those are frightening words. And so they ought to be. They point out the way we tend to treat Jesus when we allow works *for* Him to become more important than relationship *with* Him. Responsibility without passion. Forgetting our first love.

Returning to first love will always come back to

Intimacy

Heart

Relationship

Passion

And so the Bridegroom steps in. "My Beloved," He says, "I don't want you to only *do* for Me. I want you to want *Me*. I want you to spend time with *Me*! I want you to talk to *Me*. I don't want dinner prepared out of duty. I'm not just looking for works. I don't want you to spend time with me 'because you have to.' Come back. Come back to your first love!"

> *They shall be My people, and I will be their God,*
> *for they shall return to Me with their whole heart.*[5]

> *My beloved spoke, and said to me:*
> *"Rise up, my love, my fair one, and come away."*[6]

Learn by Heart

There will always be a response to passion, but there will not always be passion in responsibility. We have to start at the right end of this equation for our relationship with the Lord to reach its full potential, for passion to flow in our lives and for *first love* to be the daily environment in which we live. In this letter to the Ephesians, there are three things we are called to do to see first love renewed in our lives. The first of these is remembering.

We've all seen the romantic movie where a couple has grown apart, and through a series of circumstances come to remember why they fell in love in the first place. He remembers her smile; she remembers his eyes. He remembers her courage; she remembers his strength. They remember the joys they've shared, the hardships they've overcome and the victories they've won. Eventually, they realize that what they have built together is worth fighting for. But it happened because they remembered.

A synonym for "remembering" is "to learn by heart." Do you remember saying that as a kid? You learned your times tables "by heart"—meaning that the knowledge was so much a part of you that it was automatic. You had that information down cold—whether it was reciting the alphabet, figuring area or naming the constellations. In the same way, we need to apply "knowing by heart" to people—knowing them so well that you trust them unreservedly, know their intents and motives, understand their weaknesses and strengths, embrace their vision and support their goals.

What do we need to remember about Jesus? Do we know Him by heart? We start to learn by heart by remembering what He has done for us. While we are always called to fresh victory and fresh encounter with Him every day, it is in remembering His past faithfulness and miracle working in our lives that gives us hope and vision and faith for the future. And for *today*.

With regularity, Scripture calls us to remember—to think on His mighty works,[7] to remember His words,[8] and to remember our testimony.[9] Remembering culminates around His table: "He took bread, gave thanks and broke it, and gave it to them, saying, 'This is My body which is given for you; do this in remembrance of Me.'"[10]

It's good to remember.

But what are we remembering? So often we come to the Lord's Table and make it about us: "*My* sin put Him on the cross. If it weren't for *me*, He wouldn't have had to do that. *I'm* so bad." And that is true—our sin *did* put Him on the cross. But that isn't what He asked us to do. He asked us to remember *Him*.

I lay down My life that I may take it again.
No one takes it from Me, but I lay it down of Myself.[11]

> But now Christ is risen from the dead,
> and has become the firstfruits of those who have fallen asleep. . . .
> For He must reign till He has put all enemies under His feet.
> The last enemy that will be destroyed is death.
> For "He has put all things under His feet."[12]

> Therefore He says:
> "When He ascended on high, He led captivity captive,
> And gave gifts to men."[13]

Our salvation, our redemption, our deliverance, our potential and our future are all released from His hand because of His death on the cross. While it's true that sin put Him there, the fact is that Jesus was not the "victim." He went to the cross as a conqueror. We need to remember Him.

In all the remembering, He remembers us too. In fact, Malachi wrote that "a book of remembrance was written before Him for those who fear the LORD and who meditate on His name."[14] Further, just as the Lord called to His people to bind His commands on their hands,[15] He says that we are engraved on His hands.[16] We think on Him, and He thinks on us.

He knows us by heart.

The other day, I came across an old Valentine that I sent to Scott. In it I reiterated things that he had done that I loved. And now, about 20 years later, I had forgotten.

Love Letter

You do things that make me keep loving you more! . . . like bringing flowers, like long walks, like cooking with me, like purple sweaters, like holding me in the morning, like letting me be on your team, like whistling at me from across the street, like throwing papers over the partition, like bags of non-allergy potato chips, like constant encouragement . . .

rLb to sgb, 1990

Rereading that card brought a smile to my face, reminded me of things I had forgotten, made me thankful again for a great gift, and put joy in my heart.

It's good to remember.

What do you remember about Jesus? What did He lift you out of? How has He healed you? How did He woo you to salvation? It's easy to get lost in your To Do list, but Jesus calls, "Remember. Remember why you started down this road in the first place. Remember what I have done for you. Remember."

Stop right now and remember. Remember what Jesus has done. Remember the deliverance He has worked in your life. Remember the surprises that He has crossed your path with. Remember Scripture that He has made alive to your heart. Remember the promises He has fulfilled.

It's good to remember!

Can't Take My Eyes Off of You

What does repentance look like to you?

I suppose it has something to do with what you are repenting of. When we come to salvation, "repentance" is confessing our sin and our need of a savior. In a family context, however, repentance may be an apology. But the word used throughout the New Testament gives us a broader understanding. It literally means to *rethink*. In other words, think again about the way you're walking. Think again about the thoughts you're thinking. Think again about the attitudes you're allowing to dominate your heart. Think again about the habits you've allowed to become a part of your everyday life.

Repentance, then, means
To change your focus,
To think a new way,
To embrace another vision,
To head in a different direction.
Repent.

This is the second thing the Ephesian church was called to do. But what were they repenting for? In regard to their works, they appeared to be doing everything right. Were they just saying "sorry" for the loss of passion? I don't think so. Passion has to do with the heart, and while that needed to change, repentance is different. Repentance has to do with focus. The Ephesians had been busy focusing on their hands—the things they were doing. Now they were being called to rethink, refocus, head in a different direction. They were being called to keep their eyes on Jesus.

Have you ever noticed that you can communicate with your eyes? My husband and I could communicate an entire conversation across a crowded room! With my children, one of "those looks" could stop them in their tracks. When we were out and about, if my kids kept their eyes on me, they would know in which direction we were heading.

I have friends who used to be farmers. Many times I have heard them relate an example of how to plow straight. You can't look right in front of the tractor because you get too tied down to the details—like the Ephesians. Instead, you have to aim at a fixed point on the horizon. When you keep your eyes "up" and not "down" you head in the right direction. In fact, the quality of the work was determined by what they were looking at.

God wants to communicate with us the same way, but in order to do that, our eyes have to be on Him. One of my favorite verses of Scripture says just that. In this passage, Israel is facing an assault that could bring them to annihilation. Hezekiah, the king, prays, "Lord, if You don't do something, this is the end of us. We don't know what to do; and we don't know what You will do. But . . . *our eyes are on You*."[17]

Another way to understand repentance is to ask: Which way am I headed? Author Kenda Creasy Dean writes of a conversation she had with an African Christian. " 'You Americans think of Christianity as a farm with a fence. Your question is, 'Are you inside the fence or outside of it?' We Africans think differently. We think of Christianity as a farm with no fence. Our question is, 'Are you heading towards the farm, or away from it?' The church's identity is not defined primarily by its edges, but by its *center*: focused on Christ . . ."[18]

True repentance challenges our focus, our center, our direction, *where we're headed*. In the case of the Ephesians, repentance required a different perspective, because they weren't "bad people doing bad things." They were people who wanted to serve Jesus and please the Father.

But they had lost focus.

So Jesus called them—and He calls us—to come back to our true center. You're doing great things; don't stop. You're standing strong; keep it up. But repent and refocus.

Our eyes are on You.

Watermelon Hearts

The Ephesians were challenged because they had forgotten "first love," but now they were being called back to "first works." The two must be related: First works show where first love lies; first love flows into first works. But what are "first works"?

Mary and Martha give us a great picture of what that looks like. Most of us have heard teachings on Mary and Martha, and we get it, don't we? We want to be like Mary, and we don't want to be like Martha. But . . . honestly, if Martha wasn't doing what she was doing, how *was* dinner going to get on the table? When Jesus and 12 dusty disciples descended on the house, hospitality was Martha's first order of business. And who can blame her?

Showing hospitality wasn't Martha's problem. There was nothing wrong with what Martha was doing. Her problem was that she was serving Jesus with her hands and not her heart. The Bible says that she was *distracted* by many things.[19] The word used means "to be over-occupied about a thing."

Maybe Martha was too focused on perfectionism—too concerned with the house being perfect and the dinner being lavish, and (oh my goodness!) look at that spot on the wall! Maybe she was feeling a bit self-important that Jesus was coming to her house. Maybe she was too proud to ask for help. Until, of course, Mary didn't offer. And then she was asking for help, hoping that Jesus would reprimand Mary.

When Jesus speaks to Martha, we again view it only as a reprimand. But it was also an invitation. "We don't need roast lamb today, Martha; peanut butter sandwiches will do. You don't need to freshen up the paint on the windowsills. There will always be dust bunnies under the sofa. There is a time to do all of that; but today—today—is about us."

Come away, My beloved.

Well-meaning Martha—busy with her works but forgetting the heart. Like the Ephesians. Like us. This isn't an issue about loveless people; it's an issue about diligent people. Martha didn't love Jesus less than Mary; she just sought to show it by doing. As a result, she was distracted by many things. She put her energy into works. What Martha completely misunderstood is that the starting place for anything in life is always at Jesus' feet, always based in relationship, always about passion.

So what do first works look like? I'm not sure that they don't look like responsibility. The Lord calls us not to change the works we're doing but to change the passion with which we are doing them.

There was a season in my life, when all the kids were (finally!) in school, that I wanted to go back to work. After all, being home by myself for the larger part of the day was—well—kind of boring. As with all of our decisions, Scott and I decided to pray about it and think about it for a few days. I was excited because there was an opening on our church staff doing something I loved and for which I was qualified.

What happened wasn't at all what I'd expected. Rather than opening a new door of ministry for me, the Lord renewed my sense of vision and purpose for the ministry I already had—my home and what I was doing in it. He brought me back to first works . . . first love.

He reminded me that the reason I had opted to be a stay-at-home mom wasn't because I couldn't think of anything else to do with my time.

- It was because I believed that my hands of blessing on our physical belongings communicated love and eternal value to those living in my home.
- I believed that my presence in our home, and the rivers of living water that Jesus caused to flow from me, filled our home with worship and materially changed the atmosphere in that dwelling.
- I believed that when I cleaned, I was doing more than just getting rid of dirt. I was creating a place of order and peace and beauty that invited God's presence. Because He is not the author of confusion,[20] I wanted to contribute to creating a place of beauty and order where He could live in our midst.
- I believed that picking up my kids at school gave me a first peek into the events of the day. They were more likely to talk then than at any other time.

· I believed that the input I had in my children's lives, and my immediate availability to them every day, allowed me the ultimate discipling opportunity. And I was completely committed to raising the next generation of God's people.
· And I believed that my husband's being able to come home to a place of peace was worth more than what I could earn.

This decision wasn't "put upon me" by Scott, nor was it anything intended to "keep me in my place." I knew that I was flying in the face of all that our culture values. Some churches tell women they can only stay home. I don't believe that either. I believe that whatever your life looks like, it should be done as unto the Lord. First love. First works.

"Stay-at-home" isn't for everyone; neither is "working mom." I would get the chance to pursue my personal dreams and goals, too; and in the years before my kids graduated high school, I would publish four books, get my master's degree and speak around the world.

But at *that* moment, I needed to be reminded that I was doing something no one else could do—and I was doing it with mission and purpose and call. I counted; I counted right where I was. And I needed to be reminded of the first love behind the first works.

I announced my decision that night at dinner. As corny as this may sound, along with meatloaf and baked potatoes, I served watermelon that I had cut into heart shapes. My heart was at home doing first works.

Passion Fruit

Can you call first works, passion fruit? I hope so! Because I want everything I do to flow from my love for Jesus Christ. The Bible tells us that whatever we do, we are to work at it with all our souls, as to the Lord and not to men,[21] and that we have been created in Christ Jesus for good works.[22]

But wait a minute. Wasn't "works" the problem in the first place? No—not if it's flowing from passion. Interestingly, while Martha was "distracted" (over-occupied with a thing), the word that is translated "works" means "that with which one is occupied." So may I ask: With what are you occupied—the person or the task? Passion or duty? Relationship or responsibility? These aren't new questions. Jesus challenged Peter with this same idea one morning on the shore of Galilee.[23]

Do you love Me?

Peter had fled to Galilee following Jesus' crucifixion and resurrection. In his own confusion over what was going on, he just . . . went back to work. Following Jesus had been great, but now He was gone. When Peter didn't know what to do next, he defaulted to what he did know. Work.

Thankfully, Jesus met Peter in the middle of his own questioning but brought the issue immediately to the point. *Do you love Me, Peter?* Then, having reestablished passion, He redefined Peter's future. *Feed My sheep.*

Jesus still asks that question of us. And He still reminds us that we can't work for Him without first loving Him.

Do you love Me? Feed my sheep.
First love. First works.

1. Revelation 2:1-7.
2. The subheadings in our Bibles are not part of the original text of Scripture. They are simply given to help us stay focused on what is happening and to break up the chapters into "bite-sized pieces" for us to read.
3. See 1 Samuel 16:7.
4. Matthew 7:22-23.
5. Jeremiah 24:7.
6. Song of Solomon 2:10.
7. See Deuteronomy 32:7; 1 Chronicles 16:12.
8. See John 16:4.
9. See Deuteronomy 6:21; Revelation 12:11.
10. Luke 22:19.
11. John 10:17-18.
12. 1 Corinthians 15:20,25-27.
13. Ephesians 4:8.
14. Malachi 3:16.
15. See Deuteronomy 6:8.
16. See Isaiah 49:16.
17. See 2 Chronicles 20.
18. Kendra Creasy Dean, *Almost Christian: What the Faith of Our Teenagers Is Telling the American Church* (Oxford, UK: Oxford University Press, 2010), p. 65.
19. See Luke 10:40.
20. See 1 Corinthians 14:33.
21. See Colossians 3:23.
22. See Ephesians 2:10.
23. See John 21:1-19.

Encountering Him

HEART JOURNAL

Even a casual glance through the Old Testament is all we need to discover how easy it is for the people of God to forget His wonderful works. Look at Exodus alone! How in the world could Israel have forgotten God's works when there was manna—every day? How could they forget when a pillar of fire towered over the Tabernacle—every day? How could they forget when there was miraculous water in a dry and desolate wilderness—every day? How could they possibly *forget*?

And how could the Ephesians have forgotten? Acts 19 describes the miraculous entry of God into that pagan city. There had been miracles, renouncing of pagan practices, a riot in the city over the entry of God's word. How could they possibly forget?

How could we possibly forget?

And yet we do. Like it or not, we forget or become "used to" God in our lives. Shocking, isn't it? And then He has to remind us:

Remember. Repent. Refocus.

One way I have found to do those three things is to regularly evaluate my life in the Lord. How much time do I spend thanking Him and appreciating what He is doing in my life? How often do I stop to consider and repent of actions or attitudes that have no place in my life?

People do these things in a number of ways. Some are in an accountability group; others may write in a journal. There are those who do something like this daily; others may do it weekly, monthly or even annually. A way that works for me is that each night when I get into bed I review my day, find five things to thank the Lord for and five things I need to repent for. It helps me to remember, repent and stay caught up with the Lord.

Try it. Tonight, get in bed and think of five things the Lord did today. It's not always that easy, because we are often oblivious to all the things He does. Then think of five things that you need to repent

of—from misusing time, to yelling at the kids, to confessing disobedience—we all have things every day that need to be covered by Him.
End your time by asking Him to help you stay on the growing edge of
walking with Him so that you do better tomorrow. We all need to remember and repent.

While I think that my "five things" is easy to remember and do,
John Wesley provided a list of compelling questions to help people
evaluate their lives and where they are in their walk with Jesus. Perhaps you will find these questions helpful as well. They can be pretty
intense. This evaluation process took me days to go through the
first time I did it!

John Wesley's Evaluation and Accountability Questions

1. Am I consciously or unconsciously creating the impression that I am better than I really am? In other words, am I a hypocrite?
2. Am I honest in all my acts and words, or do I exaggerate?
3. Do I confidently pass on to another what I was told in confidence?
4. Can I be trusted?
5. Am I a slave to dress, friends, work or habits?
6. Am I self-conscious, self-pitying or self-justifying?
7. Did the Bible live in me today?
8. Do I give it time to speak to me every day?
9. Am I enjoying prayer?
10. When did I last speak to someone else of my faith?
11. Do I pray about the money I spend?
12. Do I get to bed on time and get up on time?
13. Do I disobey God in anything?
14. Do I insist upon doing something about which my conscience is uneasy?
15. Am I defeated in any part of my life?
16. Am I jealous, impure, critical, irritable, touchy or distrustful?
17. How do I spend my spare time?
18. Am I proud?
19. Do I thank God that I am not as other people, especially as the Pharisees who despised the publican?
20. Is there anyone who I fear, dislike, disown, criticize, hold resentment toward or disregard? If so, what am I doing about it?
21. Do I grumble or complain constantly?
22. Is Christ real to me?

THE CHOICE

Brian and Melissa knew each other in high school but had never thought of each other as friends. They had served on student council together. (In fact, Brian voted against her when she ran for office!) They were both on the track team together. He played basketball; she was a cheerleader. But they were in different grades, which at that age is a big deal. They were born the same year, but the dates of their birthdays put Melissa a grade ahead of Brian.

So, though they were acquaintances, they were not friends.

Until college.

Brian and Melissa attended The King's University, a Bible college and seminary founded in 1997. They began school just two years later, and because of the newness of the school, it was then attracting primarily commuter students—people already established in families and ministries. At that point, there were so few students in the late-teens-early-20s category that those who were in that age group became friends almost by default! Such was the early story of Brian and Melissa. They had many of the same classes and occasionally did homework together. They went to the same Bible study group. They talked all the time. They were getting to know each other.

One day, Brian recounts that he saw Melissa walking across the campus and he heard the Holy Spirit whisper into his heart, *"That's the girl you're going to marry."*

Brian's immediate response was, "I'm not telling *anyone* that! They'll think I'm crazy!"

I completely understand that response. You don't have to walk in Christian circles for very long before you bump into someone who tells you that "God told them" who their spouse will be. So before we continue with Brian and Melissa's story, let me address that topic. I obviously believe that God can tell people who their spouse will be—it happened to my son. However, I *don't* believe that it happens nearly as often as people think, so allow me to note a couple of guidelines in that regard.

First, we could all learn a lot by doing what Mary did when she "kept all these things and pondered them in her heart."[1] We are so quick to tell people everything we think we've heard from God, when in reality we need to pray and ponder, wait and see, go forward and let life unfold. If you think the Lord has said something like that to you—keep it to yourself, pray about it and let God direct your steps . . . and the steps of the other person. I have watched too many people put their lives on hold because they believe they have heard the voice of God in this regard. If it's Him, He will do it—you won't have to. And if nothing is happening . . . move on with your life.

I've sadly watched people wait for years, pursuing nothing else in their lives while they have waited for something that never materialized. One woman clung to a "word" for over a decade. She never even went out with the gentleman in question. There was *never* anything between them. But she steadily refused to go out with anyone else, though she was asked. So let me repeat: *If it's God, He will do it—you won't have to. And if nothing is happening . . . it wasn't the Lord. Move on with your life.*

Second, we make little room for the fact that everyone has a free will. *Even if* God has spoken to you, it is His job, not yours, to speak to the other person. I have known people who think that God has spoken to them, so they go and tell the other individual. Simply put, that is "spiritual manipulation." God doesn't make any of us into robots at salvation who now just follow a predefined program of events. We are on a journey with Him, and He unfolds it for us each step of the way. We are simply called to obey Him today and not worry about tomorrow.[2] And the other person has the right to make his or her own decision as well. It's a dangerous place to presume that we can force someone into action because we think we've heard God. If it is truly the Lord, He will do it—you won't have to. (Where have I heard that recently?)

Third, find a mentor—preferably of the same gender as you. Find someone that you know to be a spiritually mature person. (I wouldn't recommend telling this kind of thing to your "pals.") But choose a person with whom you can be honest and accountable. I usually hear these kinds of "God told me my spouse" statements from women. To be honest, I would be more inclined to believe it coming from a guy, because they're the ones who are to lead the relationship. They're the ones who are supposed to engage the pursuit. This is a simple acknowledgment of how God tends to work. While the Bible never says that "all women are supposed to submit to all men," it does say that within the marriage relationship, wives are supposed to submit to their husbands. It stands to reason, then, that if God wants to put two people together, He will do it in a way that sets the foundation in place for a lifetime of successful relationship.

While I don't think women are supposed to sit at home hoping the phone rings (for goodness' sake, get a life!), neither do I think that we are to chase down prospects. And, gentlemen . . . don't be afraid to be bold! God will give vision and command action to the one who is supposed to take action. (That's you!)

And such was the case with Brian . . . sort of.

He and Melissa were already getting to know each other, and now he was ready to pursue something more. But being an earnest and obedient disciple of Jesus Christ, he asked the Lord, "Can I ask her out?" Another point of wisdom! We so often assume that if we hear something from the Lord, we are to immediately leap into action! Brian wisely asked for the next step. *Can I ask her out?*

The surprising answer? No.

Brian relayed this story to me years after he and Melissa were married. He said that he asked the Lord that question every day for a year. *Can I ask her out?* With the same response—no.

On Melissa's side of the story, interest between the two of them was obviously growing, and she couldn't figure out why Brian wouldn't ask her out. She, of course, knew nothing of God's dealings with Brian, and so she was becoming more and more frustrated. To her, it simply looked like he was procrastinating, when in fact, he was waiting for the "go ahead" from the Lord. Timing is everything.

Brian knew the end of the story before it had begun. Though he pondered in his heart, he believed that the Lord had told him to pursue that girl. *But he valued obedience more.*

Can I say that again? *He valued obedience more.* Obedience that listens for *today.* Obedience that waits on the Lord. Obedience that recognizes that if He orders our steps that means every step.

Time went by. Brian and Melissa became one another's best friends. Then, the day finally arrived when the Lord said, "YES!" Brian asked her out on a romantic date to a little Italian place.

rebecca hayford bauer · www.regalbooks.com

And the choice was made.

He had learned obedience. She had learned patience. And they had both learned faithfulness to walking out the path the Lord set before them.

....

I have often had people ask me how Scott and I were able to maintain a happy, successful, connected and passionate marriage—while working, going to school, raising a family and being in ministry.

I have come to firmly believe that successful marriages are based first in radical discipleship and then in radical commitment. I lived this out in my life by making two choices every day—I chose Jesus, and I chose Scott.

Every day, I made the choice for Jesus again. I'm not talking about "getting saved" over and over. I'm talking about consistently challenging the human tendency to compromise, accept mediocrity or become passive about—well—anything. I have certainly had moments when those behaviors crept into my life with the Lord.

You know how that goes, don't you? One day you suddenly open your eyes and realize that you need to reevaluate some things in your life. It's a moment to open your heart and allow Him to search you and see if there is any sinful way in you.[3] It's a time to allow Him to clean up and re-target your life.

In my own walk, I have found that it's easier in the long run to do that every day and stay on track rather than have to make a major course correction a couple of times each year.

Jesus . . . today . . . I choose You again. I choose to love You. I choose to serve You. I choose to let You change my life. I'm my Beloved's, and He is mine. You are "first and last, best and most" in my life. You are my God. You are my Savior. You are my Lord.

And then I would do the same thing in regard to Scott.

Today . . . I choose you . . . again. I choose to love you and serve you and submit to you. I choose to partner with you in the mission God has given us. I choose to embrace beliefs, goals, lifestyle, purpose and calling with you. When things get hard, I choose us. When money is in short supply, I choose us. When we can't seem to get along, I promise to work it out. When it feels like everything is going wrong, I will stay. I choose *us*.

The choice to choose one another is ultimately no different than the choice to choose Jesus.

> Commitment
>> Covenant
>>> Faithfulness

Scott made the same choices each day too. Jesus was absolutely first. A threefold covenant between Jesus, Scott and me. This was more than wanting to play house; this was more than wanting to have a family. This was a promise, in front of Jesus, to commit to our marriage and reaffirm that we really meant the things we said in our wedding vows:

> richer, poorer
>> sickness, health
>>> forsaking all others
>>>> until death do us part

It's the same choice the church at Smyrna had to make.

Be faithful until death.

They were facing persecution from both the pagan population and from Jewish opponents. Things weren't looking like what they thought they would. They had made a choice to serve Jesus, and now they were having to make it again.

Jesus . . . today . . . I choose You again.

....

When it comes to walking with the Lord and growing in Him, we get a thousand choices a day—from how we talk (will we give in to telling that shady story, or let a curse escape our lips?), to what we watch (does our entertainment support what we believe? Or are we watching things that compromise us in secret?), to what we eat (do we *really* believe that our bodies are the temple of the Holy Spirit?), to how we manage our emotions, face difficulty, deal with money, raise our children . . . and the list could go on. When it comes right down to it, *everything* about our lives should reflect our choice to follow Him.

Yes—every new day presents us with thousands of choices. Once Jesus is in our life, all of those choices must be guided by Him as surely as a bride makes her choices based on the desires of her beloved. He has chosen us; now our lives must show that we are choosing Him. Every day.

To the angel of the church in Smyrna write: "These are the words of him who is the First and the Last, who died and came to life again. 'I know your afflictions and your poverty—yet you are rich! I know the slander of those who say they are Jews and are not, but are a synagogue of Satan. Do not be afraid of what you are about to suffer. I tell you, the devil will put some of you in prison to test you, and you will suffer persecution for ten days. Be faithful, even to the point of death, and I will give you the crown of life. He who has an ear, let them hear what the Spirit says to the churches. He who overcomes will not be hurt at all by the second death.' "[4]

Home Improvements

The quality of the foundation of any building is of critical importance. The same is true of any life or any relationship. It has to be built on more than mere emotion. As important as passion is, emotion isn't enough to get you through the long haul. There must be a solid foundation in your life. I once heard someone teaching on the topic of choosing a life partner. This person said, "You know how in real estate it's all about location, location, location? Well, when it comes to choosing a husband or a wife, it's all about character, character, character."

The dictionary defines "character" as "moral excellence and firmness." In other words, people of character are those who are firm in what they believe. There is a resolve about how they live. They have made a choice and they will not swerve from it, nor will they compromise. They are rock-solid people you can build your life with . . . and on.

Kind of like Jesus.

In fact, in Matthew 7, Jesus describes two people—one who built his life on sand, one who built his life on rock. Metaphorically speaking, Jesus is the rock.[5] We are safe if we build on Him. *His* character is rock solid! But as in the story, you only find out the strength of who a person is and what he or she has built on when difficulty arises. Standing firm in what you believe is easy when everything is going well. But what about when times get tough? That's when you find out about a person's character. "If you fall to pieces in a crisis, there wasn't much to you in the first place."[6]

Our choices will always be tested, just as surely as our choices for the Lord are challenged by our adversary, the devil; by the culture around us; by temptation. Taking a stand will always invite opposition. The church in Smyrna found that out.

Brian and Melissa found that out too.

As their relationship continued to develop, another young man decided he was going to make a play for Melissa. At the same time, someone else decided that Brian would be the perfect choice for their daughter. While these actions didn't divide Brian and Melissa, the distraction and potential for division and discord were there. *Was Melissa inviting or encouraging this guy's attentions? Was Brian looking for a back-up plan in case this plan didn't work out?* These are questions they had to grapple with and then determine if they trusted each other. They had to decide if they were making a life-choice or if they were still just playing around at dating.

These situations took their relationship to a whole new level. They learned to be unified in their commitment, to trust each other's intentions and to stand—together—against other intrusions. In doing so, Brian and Melissa strengthened their determination to stand up for what they believed to be their future—each other.

It could have been different. Either of those situations could have brought a division between the two of them that might have ended the relationship. Instead they learned to walk in

Unity. Trust. Faithfulness. Belief. Hope. A future.

Which brings us back to our relationship with the Lord. What do we do with the things and circumstances of life? Do we choose the "easy road" that the world *always* offers? Temptations will constantly surround us, beckoning with false hope that there just might be something better out there. Everything around you—from the adversary to advertising—holds out an illusion, an image, a fantasy designed to breed dissatisfaction with you, your life, who's in it, and what's in it. You can spend your life chasing shadows, always hoping that perfection is around the corner or in the next relationship. You can invest in shadows, or you can invest in the reality that God brings into your life. That kind of reality—real people, growing in Him just like you are—can grow into genuine relationship, true love, unswerving commitment and depth of character.

The good news is that character is learned. Character is practiced. Character is chosen. If learning to live as a person of "moral excellence and firmness" isn't something that you grew up with or had discipled into you, the process is described in Scripture: "So don't lose a minute in building on what you've been given, complementing your basic faith with good character, spiritual understanding, alert discipline, passionate patience, reverent wonder, warm friendliness, and generous love, each dimension fitting into and developing the others."[7]

But it doesn't come without the choice. And it doesn't come without the challenge.

Our culture and our adversary the devil are relentless in seeking to divide us from the Lord. Temptations arise that invite compromise. Doubt infiltrates the mind. Life gangs up on you, and in sheer weariness you give in or give up or give out.

In the middle of it all, Jesus whispers His vows of

life and life more abundant,[8]

joy beyond measure,[9]

peace that passes all understanding.[10]

His proven character backs up those promises, and our character is challenged to grow and stay true to our choice.

Be faithful until death . . .

Commitment Issues

The idea of "being faithful unto death" seems like a fairy tale in our broken world—and we tend to cast a skeptical eye at "happy endings." When did we become afraid to love, afraid to choose, afraid to give our hearts?

Probably when we didn't "get chosen."

All of us have suffered the hurt, disappointment and rejection of not being chosen. Not being chosen may have involved a team, a parent, a job or a relationship. Not being chosen is painful. And from that point on, we feared making ourselves vulnerable again, trusting again. I'm convinced that the residual fear of past experiences is the biggest challenge to our making choices today. Each time we have to make a choice, we subconsciously start weighing every option, looking at every angle and analyzing everyone's opinions.

And when it comes to relationships, we become afraid to make the choice—not the choice to date, but the choice to commit.

We even do it with Jesus.

Ah—commitment, the theme of so many sitcoms; the topic of relationship advice; the complaint of every disillusioned female whose boyfriend hasn't popped the question. *"He has commitment issues."* Whether he does or doesn't isn't the point here. The question is . . .

Do you have commitment issues?

When it comes to Jesus Christ our Bridegroom, are we fully committed?

"Commitment" can be defined as a promise, pledge or vow; dedication, loyalty, devotion, steadfastness, faithfulness. One author describes this investment in relationship as "a chance to be deeply known."[11] Talk about vulnerability! That's just a little terrifying, isn't it? No wonder we're afraid of commitment. No wonder we have commitment issues.

Though we long for love, we fear love. We fear making that deep commitment, the finality of choosing. What's more, we fear that once chosen, the chosen one will choose to leave us. And many of us have reason to fear that love will go away. Not only have we possibly experienced it, but it's also deeply rooted in our culture. Just listen to our language! We say that love has died or grown cold. Music proclaims love's demise with "you don't bring me flowers anymore." Couples say, "we've grown apart." And someone who has a break-up is "unlucky in love." Hardship in relationships is explained with the phrase, "When poverty comes in the door, loves flies out the window." There is no commitment, no lasting relationship, no one you can count on. And many of us have experienced that.

But we're dealing with a different Bridegroom now.

This is One like no other.

Jesus *defines* commitment. It is He who looks deeply into our eyes and promises to never leave. He promises to never stop loving us.

Author Daniel Brown writes, "God yearns for us. It thrills him to fully disclose himself to us. At the heart of our relationship with God is knowing him and being known by him. We, too, want to be known and to truly know other people. Some people run from relationship to relationship, looking for that person who will understand them. The truth is that the only one who can do that completely and redemptively is God himself. If we cut him out of our life's equation, we will always long for some deeper comfort, some deeper commitment."[12]

Have you ever watched a couple get to know each other? Of course you have! We've all seen it. We've all done it. Romance hits, and suddenly, in the desire to please the beloved, they begin to take an interest in things they were never interested in before. Guys dress a little nicer; girls suddenly know the rules of hockey. Guys bring flowers; girls wear his favorite color. Guys look for tickets to the ballet; girls agree to go to the demolition derby.

What happened? Love.

But as time passes, those surface interests—important though they are—begin to get set aside in favor of *really knowing* the heart of the beloved. The couple moves beyond simply knowing one another's likes and dislikes to knowing one another's hearts—understanding motives, embracing visions, sharing heartaches, celebrating strengths, and accepting weaknesses. Really knowing someone will involve

Time. Vulnerability. Honesty. Trust. Commitment.

A "guy" moves to being a *man*—not seeking advantage or his own benefit, but becoming a protector and true lover, offering a place of safety in his heart. A "girl" stops being nervous around the beloved and becomes a *woman* who offers encouragement, respect and love to one who faces a harsh world every day. Love keeps going deeper. The desire to commit to one another reaches ever deepening and more intimate dimensions.

Love Letter

If love truly is found in commitment, then the harvest of years of commitment is unspeakable joy, complete devotion and an irresistible taste for tomorrow . . . with you!

sgb to rlb, undated

Love grows. Love goes deeper.

And we are called to do the same with Jesus. As we walk through each day, and His love woos our hearts, do we offer ourselves as those who are always looking out for His best interests? Are we always seeking to please Him? Or are we still at the twitter-pated, "get all excited" stage? We're called to relationship with Jesus . . . not just to "have a crush" on Him. And, as in any relationship, love will require more.

More depth.

More commitment.

More vulnerability.

For you are a holy people to the LORD your God,
and the LORD has chosen you to be a people for Himself,
a special treasure above all the peoples who are on the face of the earth.[13]

You did not choose Me, but I chose you.[14]

He has chosen us. Now our lives must show that we have chosen Him.

You and You Alone

A young couple once came to Scott and me for premarital counseling. They were struggling. He was away at school and seemed to have quite a few female friends for a guy who was engaged. His fiancée was justifiably concerned. Though he wasn't dating any of these girls, he would help them move, repair things for them, study with them or just hang out with them. In his mind, I think he truly believed he was "being a brother."

But what began to emerge in the course of our conversation was his need "to be needed," and whether intentional or not, it was being met in other women.

Red flag! Red flag!

That day at the office grew very long as this couple reevaluated everything they were planning. At one point, she returned her engagement ring. Many hours—and a lot of discussion—later, he re-proposed.

In those hours, they had made some very excellent decisions. He was going to leave college for a year to go home and spend a lot of time with his dad learning how to be a husband. They chose to delay their wedding. Two years later, however, when the wedding day finally arrived, they were ready to make that commitment. A decade and four children later, they are still doing great!

But it came at a cost.

When they postponed their marriage, reservations at the church and the reception site had already been made. The bridal party had been asked to participate. Dresses had been ordered. Though invitations had yet to go out, many people already had the date on the calendar. This was a potentially embarrassing situation. But they took the risk . . .

to discover the joy of "you and you alone."

When it comes to making the choice, you can only choose one. When we choose Jesus, we really don't have the option of mixing Him with other beliefs or other loves. Scripture tells us that we can't serve God and the world.[15] Jesus doesn't just become one of our "favorites" on the computer. He wants to be the one. The *only* one.

Moses proclaimed, "The LORD our God, the LORD is one!"[16] Both psalmist and prophet declared, "You alone are God!"[17] There is no other. People spend their whole lives longing to find "The One." And we have found Him. His name is Jesus. He desires to be "you and you alone" to each one of us. To do that, we have to make our choice.

A choice to trust the Beloved.

A choice to commit our lives.

A choice for "You and You alone."

Brian and Melissa only remembered having met in high school. But during their courtship, we discovered that they had crossed paths much earlier than that.

In elementary school, Melissa's family had briefly attended our church. During that time, the children's ministries department had put on a play called "Treasure Hunt." Ten-year-old Brian was one of the main characters—four brothers and sisters who were on an adventure. As the story moved from scene to scene, they wound up in the dark and scary forest at night. The play taught about trusting the Lord and confronting fear, so the four rolled out their sleeping bags to go to sleep and trust themselves to God's care. As they "slept," four protecting angels came out and danced around them.

One day, we were reminiscing as a family, sharing with Melissa some of Brian's "growing up" stories. Someone mentioned "Treasure Hunt." Melissa immediately said, "I was in that." We all turned and looked at her, trying to place what she did in the play, because none of us could remember her. She went on, "I was one of the angels that came out and danced around the kids in their sleeping bags." Well, we immediately broke out the "Treasure Hunt" video to see Melissa's part, and what we discovered was our own family treasure. It turned out that she was the protecting angel over Brian.

Isn't God romantic? He was making the choice long before Brian and Melissa even knew each other. And He was making the choice for us long before we ever knew Him too.[18]

---

1. Luke 2:19.
2. See Matthew 6:34.
3. See Psalm 139:23-24.
4. Revelation 2:8-11, *NIV*.
5. See 1 Corinthians 10:4.
6. Proverbs 24:10, *THE MESSAGE*.
7. 2 Peter 1:5-7, *THE MESSAGE*.
8. See John 10:10.
9. See Psalm 16:11.
10. See Philippians 4:7.
11. Daniel Brown, *Unlock the Power of Family*, self-published, 2006, p. 111.
12. Ibid., p. 114.
13. Deuteronomy 14:2.
14. John 15:16.
15. See Matthew 6:24.
16. Deuteronomy 6:4.
17. Psalm 86:10; Isaiah 37:16.
18. See Romans 5:8.

Encountering Him

HE CHOOSES ME

Throughout the Bible several things commemorate the establishing of a choice. Sometimes choice is established by building an altar, sometimes by the setting up of a stone; but it can also be established by the pouring out of oil. Look at the story of David. When he was chosen as king, it was marked by the pouring out—the anointing—of oil.[1] In the Bible, we also see that oil represents joy, healing and the breaking of yokes—that which weighs us down or holds us back.[2]

And it is symbolic of choice.

As David's story shows, the anointing of oil indicated a choice by God to bring someone into
    rulership,
        acceptance,
            destiny,
                and purpose.

All of those things are true of us too. He has chosen us, and He has plans for us! A destiny. A future. Full partnership. Ruling with Him.

If knowing—truly *knowing*—that you are chosen—"accepted in the Beloved"[3]—is an issue for you, I would like to encourage you to anoint yourself with oil as a sign that you have been chosen by the King of kings, our Bridegroom, Jesus Christ. As I just noted, not only does oil establish choice, but it also brings healing, joy and freedom where we have felt hindered in accepting acceptance.

Think about that for a moment: *accepting acceptance*. Jesus stands before us offering complete approval, access, esteem, adoration, respect, love, *acceptance*.

And we step back because we can't believe it's for us. For me. For you.

We all have moments when we default to our own unworthiness, guilt and shame. But remember, condemnation only comes from the adversary. In fact, John describes him as "the accuser." If you are ever in "default" mode, remember that Scripture teaches us that there is no condemnation to those who are in Christ Jesus.[4] The price has been paid.

There was a time in my own life when I was struggling deeply with my identity in Christ and His love for me. I knew it in my head, but I was having trouble getting it into my heart. One of the things I did daily in that time period was to anoint myself with oil each morning. It was not done superstitiously, as though the oil itself imparted anything to me. It was more like a radical reminder to myself, a practical action to press into my heart that I was God's daughter, His chosen, the Bride of Christ. The same is true for you! Allow this anointing to be a reminder that You are His beloved and that

He has chosen you!

---

1. See 1 Samuel 16:1-13.
2. See Isaiah 10:27; 61:3; James 5:14.
3. Ephesians 1:6.
4. See Romans 8:1; Revelation 12:10.

THE PROPOSAL

I still have to laugh when I think of the day my daughter got engaged.

My soon-to-be son-in-law, James, knew that Lindsey was trying to figure out when he was going to propose. Their relationship had reached a stage that it was no longer a question of "if," but "when."

Even so, he was determined that the proposal be a complete surprise.

He began making his plan weeks in advance; but in order to pull off the surprise, he needed me as an accomplice.

He created a very realistic-looking invitation for a fabricated event that was supposedly being given in honor of my late husband, Scott. The awarding of this honor made my presence necessary. Our plan was that upon receiving the invitation, I would insist that Lindsey accompany me because I didn't want to go alone. She would (according to "the plan") calmly go with me, and I would get her to the right place at the right time so James could pop the question.

A foolproof plan, right?

And it might have been, except for one thing.

When I informed my daughter that she would be going with me to this "event," she was completely frustrated with me. She was an *adult*, after all. I should have given her a choice. Of course I hadn't given her a choice! I knew what was *really* going on, and I couldn't take the chance that she would turn me down! So, I bribed her with a new outfit and promised we could leave the event as early as possible. I teased her, cajoled her, challenged attitudes. In fact, I tried everything I could think of to interest her in going with me.

All to no avail. Absolutely nothing could sway her.

Before I go on, I have to give a disclaimer in defense of my daughter. I would never be able to share this story if this kind of attitude and reaction was standard practice with her. So let me give a bit more context. Right at the time all of this was going on, we were coming up on the one-year anniversary of Scott's death. This season was filled with emotion and wasn't easy on any of us. The grief journey over the loss of her dad was long, and she had no desire at all to go to another event that would surface all of that again.

Well, despite everything, the big day finally arrived, and her attitude hadn't improved. She *did* wear her new outfit but refused to put on makeup. (Boy, was *she* sorry later!) She complained the entire drive. Nothing was going to change her mind about this. She didn't want to go, and she wanted to make sure I knew that. Personally speaking, however, my favorite line of the whole evening came as we were driving to the rendezvous spot. She uttered the words, "This is the worst day of my life!"

I could hardly keep from cracking up!

When we arrived, James was standing outside looking pretty dapper—dressed up, nice suit, holding a single red rose—waiting for his beloved . . . whose attitude miraculously and instantly changed! I left—mission accomplished. James popped the question. Lindsey said yes.

And we had a beautiful wedding the following summer.

....

Several years before my daughter's wedding, I had received my own proposal—from Jesus. In the summer of 2003, for a period of about three months, every morning when I awoke and my feet hit the floor, the Lord would say to my heart, *"Will you marry Me?"*

Obviously, I knew what the words logically meant. I even knew what they biblically meant. He's the Bridegroom; we're the Bride. What I *didn't know* was what He was asking. What did He want me to *do* with what He was saying?

In retrospect, I would understand that it was part of God's gracious preparation of my heart for the home-going of my husband. Scott went to be with the Lord just a few months following the experience described above. In the void of Scott's absence, Jesus stepped in and became my husband. And all summer long, He had been wooing my heart.

God promises to be your husband.[1]

Scripture makes that promise to the woman alone; and I had quoted that verse to women before. Now people were quoting it to me, and I wasn't sure I liked it. Truthfully, how many of us, when deprived of something physical and tangible are happy to exchange it for something spiritual and invisible? Are we ready and willing to allow God to "make up the difference" in our lives? I can only say that I wasn't ready for that any more than anyone else would be. But in the months following Scott's death, I discovered how true that verse was, and how truly the Lord becomes everything we need. I learned

> how closely Jesus wants to hold us,
> > how intimately He wants to know us,
> > > how near He wants His presence to be to us.

You don't have to walk the same road I did in order to learn that. In fact, I hope you don't. But to each one of us, Jesus issues the invitation:

> Will you marry Me?
> > I want a deeper relationship with you.
> > > Behold, I stand at the door and knock.

Have you ever looked closely at that verse? Most of the time it's quoted when someone is being invited to accept salvation in Jesus Christ. But remember, these letters were written to people who had already made that decision. This verse was written to the Church. It was written to you. It was written to me. Look at what it says:

> I'm at the door.
> > I'm knocking.
> > > I'm asking: Will you let Me in?

> If you do
> > I will come in
> > > I will eat with you.

There is something so intimate about this invitation. And in its own way, it becomes a proposal. Jesus is asking to make a home with you. He will step over the threshold of your life. You'll eat meals together. It's homey, it's intimate, it's the two of you.

> *It's a proposal.*

Like many significant moments in our life, a proposal represents the ending of one thing and the beginning of another. It's why those transitional moments—high school graduation, moving, changing schools—are so bittersweet. While something wonderful is beginning, life will never be the same again. Transition.

A proposal is a similar transition. It is the ending of a dating relationship and the beginning of two people melding into one, preparing to create a home and family, building the foundation of a life together. A proposal launches a season of intentionality, definition and commitment. Things you may have been patient with in a friend or even in a dating relationship now come up for review. Things you never would have discussed or cared about become major topics of conversation.

I once did the premarital counseling for a young couple that kept insisting to me that ever since they got engaged all they did was argue. I was equally insistent in telling them that, "No, you're not arguing; you're defining."

One such defining moment that Scott and I had early in our marriage was over ketchup storage. My mother kept it in the refrigerator; his mother kept it in the cupboard. Hence the discussion! It was the "Ketchup Controversy of '76." (By the way—the final determination was that ketchup placement should be determined by the primary cook. Though Scott was quite a good cook, the primary cook was me; so the ketchup went in the fridge.)

During courtship, you only see each other a couple of hours a week, and definition is unnecessary because the majority of the time you can continue doing everything as you always have. But now that you are moving toward marriage and creating a home together, every detail is up for definition. "Communication" is the word of the day. And you need to learn tact and diplomacy for everything. Even ketchup. Because living with another person will always press us to grow.

It's no different when we invite Jesus to come live with us. His presence will require growth, demand commitment and result in change. Building a home with Him will change our focus, redefine life as we know it, and issue forth in a companionship, intimacy and unity unknown before. That's a lot to consider when you accept a proposal!

The moment we say yes to His proposal is the moment we go from being simply a believer in Him to being a disciple. Lots of people *believe* in Jesus Christ. Lots of people have asked Him into their hearts and have received salvation. But hosts of people who believe in Jesus have yet to decide that His presence in their lives will actually bring about life-change.

They haven't yet become a disciple.

They haven't yet opened the door.

They haven't yet accepted the proposal to *build a life* with Him.

To the angel of the church in Laodicea write: "These are the words of the Amen, the faithful and true witness, the ruler of God's creation. I know your deeds, that you are neither cold nor hot. I wish you were either one or the other! So, because you are lukewarm—neither hot nor cold—I am about to spit you out of my mouth. You say, 'I am rich; I have acquired wealth and do not need a thing.' But you do not realize that you are wretched, pitiful, poor, blind and naked. I counsel you to buy from me gold refined in the fire, so you can become rich; and white clothes to wear, so you can cover your shameful nakedness; and salve to put on your eyes, so you can see. Those whom I love I rebuke and discipline. So be earnest, and repent. Here I am! I stand at the door and knock. If anyone hears my voice and opens the door, I will come in and eat with him, and he with me. To him who overcomes, I will give the right to sit with me on my throne, just as I overcame and sat down with my Father on his throne. He who has an ear, let him hear what the Spirit says to the churches."[2]

Fire and Ice

I wrestled for years over the "lukewarm" comments of this passage.

To the Laodiceans, however, it made perfect sense.

Archaeology reveals that Laodicea had an aqueduct that carried water from the hot mineral springs of Hieropolis about five miles away. Water traveling this distance would have become tepid by the time it arrived at their city.[3] Lukewarm water was common to them. It was what they had to drink—the very definition of water.

How lovely it must have been to travel to Hieropolis and enjoy the hot springs! Or to go to nearby Colossae to drink the pure, cool water from the river there. The apostle Paul mentions these three cities in Colossians 4:13. The three were, in fact, near neighbors—but not equally blessed in their water sources.

It took me years—actually decades—to finally realize what "I wish you were hot or cold" meant. Why? Because I'd always viewed "hot" as positive and "cold" as negative.

In Scripture, we see God appear to Israel in a pillar of fire; John preached a baptism of fire; and on the day of Pentecost the Holy Spirit appeared as fire. Wasn't God here to "set us on fire" so that we would go into all the world?

And maybe I just got caught up in the idioms of our culture. "Blowing hot and cold" means to change constantly, to waver or not know where you stand on something. For the life of me I couldn't figure out why Jesus would *ever* want us to be cold. More idioms please: Did He want us to have "cold feet" (doubt), break out into a "cold sweat" (fear), give Him the "cold shoulder" (rejection) or "be as cold as ice" (hardheartedness)? I just had a hard time with this.

Until one day it dawned on me that the Holy Spirit isn't only revealed as fire; He's also pictured as water. Jesus said that when the Holy Spirit comes there will be "rivers of living water"[4] pouring out of us. That sounds pretty good. Isaiah compares the pouring out of water with the pouring out of the Spirit: "For I will pour water on him who is thirsty, and floods on the dry ground; I will pour My Spirit on your descendants, and My blessing on your offspring."[5] David talks about "a river whose streams shall make glad the city of God,"[6] and all who desire are invited to come and drink. "Let him who thirsts come. Whoever desires, let him take the water of life freely."[7]

There are just times when only a cold drink will do. And other times when only a hot drink will do. Cold can be so refreshing and invigorating on a hot day! I've never been a big soda drinker, but once or twice each summer—usually on a 100-plus-degree day—only a Coke with extra ice will do the job! And in the winter—ah, hot is the ticket! Peppermint tea is tingly clear to your toes, comforting and warming when even the ends of your hair seem cold! A frothy, creamy latte is even better. (And make that an iced latte in the summer!)

Bottom line . . . lukewarm will always disappoint.

Jesus' warning against being lukewarm is a reminder that passion should never die! Whatever the situation demands, the response should also be intense and intentional, meeting the need of the circumstance—cold when you're overheated, and warm when you're freezing. A soft word in the heat of a difficult moment; encouraging words when zeal is waning. Lukewarm will always lead us to half-heartedness, lethargy and indifference. But hot or cold will always

> *build up.*
>> *support.*
>>> *encourage.*
>>>> *refresh.*
>>>>> *comfort.*

I Need You

Besides needing to challenge their lukewarmness and let passion rise again in their hearts, the church at Laodicea needed to challenge their self-sufficiency. In short, they believed they had it all. They needed nothing. They were complete. Maybe they even thought they were so pulled together that Jesus was a bit lucky to have them!

All of us are tempted to self-sufficiency. None of us wants to be thought of as emotionally needy, high maintenance, discontent, pessimistic or always having a problem. And so when we face challenges, we default to "I can handle this on my own." Our tendency is to put on the "happy church face" for Sunday and tell no one what is really happening in our lives.

But that isn't how relationships are supposed to work. Relationships are given to us for the mutual building up of each other in love and support. We can get so caught up in our own self-sufficiency that we forget how much we need one another. And we certainly forget how much we need Him.

In the process of a courtship, that's a big deal.

There is some rather faulty thinking on the part of some who view someone who is unmarried as "half" of a person running around looking for his or her other half. They forget the wholeness that we have in Christ and begin looking for someone to—as the movie so inaccurately proclaimed—"complete me." While I understand what they are saying, the Bible says that we are complete in Jesus.[8]

Scripture also tells us that when a man and woman come together in marriage, they become one.[9] The coming together as a couple creates an entirely new entity! This doesn't mean they were two halves before. No, it simply means that together they are something brand new in the world. There is a laying down of oneself for the other that forms a union—a completely new package that never existed before and is completely different than what each would have been individually. It's an exciting process, but one that requires that you recognize your need of one another.

It is no different in our relationship with the Lord Jesus. His life in ours creates newness in us. In fact, Paul declares that we become "new creatures." That will not happen, though, without Jesus at work in our lives. It won't happen without our laying down our lives for Him, remembering how He already laid down His life for us.

We need Him.

At some point in a courtship, we move beyond simply *liking* someone, simply *wanting* them. We find that we *need* them. A lot of love songs have been written about not being able to live without the beloved.

This is what the Laodiceans were being called to. When Jesus challenged them to "buy from Him," He was challenging them to take a long, hard look at their lives and see—truly *see*—the places where they needed Him. It was a challenge to give up self-sufficiency, individualism and autonomy.

And it's what *we're* being called to. Our need of Jesus rests on our ability to take that same kind of long, hard look at ourselves and freely admit that we cannot make it through a day without Him. As we prepare for His coming, as we prepare for His proposal, we must move beyond liking Jesus, or wanting Him in our life; we must

long to spend every minute with Him,

be desperate for Him,

not be able to live without Him.

Unfortunately, the opposite often seems to be the case. The longer we know Him, the more likely we are to make Him a habit. To become accustomed to His presence. To be numb to His working and dull to His voice. And that scares me, because it's exactly what the religious people did in Jesus' day.

The Pharisees. How vulnerable all of us are to becoming like them! They roundly criticized Jesus for eating with sinful people. "Don't you get it, Jesus?" they cried. "Not only are you not doing things the way we want you to (you didn't even wash your hands, for goodness' sake!), but you're eating with people who are off-the-chart lowlifes and sinners."

Really, the Pharisees weren't so different from the Laodiceans. "We don't need anything, Jesus! We're rich. The things of God and our study of Scripture have filled us with spiritual riches beyond imagining. Really, Jesus, we've got all these scrolls we read, and fancy clothes that we wear and all these amazing traditions that we follow. So life is pretty full doing our religion thing. Thanks for caring, but we don't actually need you. We're just fine."

They didn't know it and couldn't see it, but He was proposing so much more for them! In Him, there will *always* be more. He never runs out, and no matter how much we think we have, we will always need Him.

Every now and then, we need to be reminded of that. I remember a time when every time I heard songs of worship, I began to cry. Looking back now, I know what it was. The Holy Spirit was stirring my soul to never forget where my strength comes from. He is the One who empowers me, animates me, energizes me, uplifts me and fills me until I overflow. The most important purpose in my whole life is falling in love with Him again and again and again, and choosing to be desperate for Jesus every day.

Jesus ate with sinners because they recognized how much they needed Him. They knew they were not sufficient in themselves. They knew they were hungry. *And they invited Him.* The "church" people didn't make that leap, didn't extend that invitation, were unable to see their need. God forbid that we ever become so "religious" that we stop inviting Jesus to dinner . . . or opening the door the moment He knocks.

Love Changes Everything

Can you imagine being in a relationship where the other person *always* has to be right? Closely akin to self-sufficiency, the Laodiceans believed that they were "right." It's why Jesus urged them to "be earnest and repent," to pursue Him and to change the very course of their lives.

This "sure I'm right" attitude is what Scott found himself dealing with when he met me. In my defense, let me say that we met when I was only 17, and I had a whole lot of growing up left to do.

While Scott was always kind to me, there were times in our relationship when he laid down the law. One of those times was shortly after we got engaged. We were in the middle of an argument and I decided that the way to "get my way" was to threaten to give back my engagement ring. Well, it worked.

Once.

The second time I tried that, Scott just looked at me and said, "If you give that back to me, I'm keeping it." In those words, he was refusing to have a relationship based on manipulation. And he was absolutely right. I read a quote once that perfectly describes what was happening at that moment: "Love is beautiful, but it is also terrible—terrible in its determination to allow nothing blemished or unworthy to remain in the beloved."[10]

We've all heard the statement that you are never to go into marriage seeking to change the other person. I've heard heartbreaking stories of people who are sure that they would lead their unbelieving fiancé(e) to the Lord, or stop their beloved from drinking or make them "see" their faults and change them—after the wedding takes place. They put up with incredible abuse and disrespect during a courtship because they believed in the power of love to change a person. *But that's true only if it's God's love that's doing the changing.*

In this case, Scott was determined to challenge this attitude in me . . . not for his sake, but for mine. Scott wasn't out to change me for his benefit. The goal was much more far-reaching. He knew that our marriage would never reflect what it needed to if I spent my time trying to control him. And just like Jesus does with us, he was determined that nothing unworthy was to remain in his beloved. He was determined to present to the Lord a bride without spot or wrinkle.[11]

The Lord doesn't come into our lives to confront attitudes just for the fun of it. He is not arbitrary or haphazard. He always challenges us with the goal of bringing us to the full potential for which He created us. It's always to make us more and more into the image of His Son.[12] It's always to take us from glory to glory[13] and to give us a future and a hope.[14]

But here's the rub.

We have to be willing to accept the correction.

I had a bigger question facing me than winning an argument or two. *Would I submit to the leadership of my bridegroom?* You can debate with me until the end of the day on the authority and submission issue in marriage. I happen to believe it; and I have also lived it. And I know that when it's lived in the spirit of Jesus Christ, it works.

But this leads us to an even weightier question: Are we willing to let Jesus, our Bridegroom, lead? Are we willing to let Him challenge things in our lives that don't contribute to a successful future? What do we do when He challenges an attitude or asks us to do something? Do we argue? Do we have a better plan? Or do we let Him lead us?

This requires us to be willing to "be earnest and repent." It goes beyond simply saying we're sorry or feeling bad to changing how we think and how we live. Repentance can happen in a moment, but the earnest pursuit of change and growth takes a lifetime. It's a joyous road to walk when we commit to it.

When we accept the proposal.

The writer of Hebrews reminds us that discipline and correction are always for a purpose—they yield the peaceful fruit of righteousness to those who have been trained by them.[15] That wording implies, though, that it's possible for a person to endure painful correction and *not* be trained by it.

What will you choose? We each have the choice of resisting His correction or making the faith-leap into it. The choice can be scary or exciting, depending on how we view our relationship with Him. If we believe that He is just out to *take* from us, then, yes—it will be scary. But if we've built our relationship with Jesus on the belief that He only does things for our good, then life-change (even when it's clothed in correction) becomes very exciting!

Just Say Yes

So what will you say when He pops the question? When He knocks at the door? When He challenges you to grow?

I have to admit that "no" used to be my standard answer to just about everything. Not because I wanted to be contrary, but because it was the safe answer. It showed up the most, though, when I was raising my children. If I said no to my children, then my life fit into a nice, neat little box. There was no risk, and no growth, perhaps, but I knew what to expect. I knew where everyone was. I knew what they were doing. I knew they were safe.

Enter Scott Bauer. He challenged me to "say yes as often as you can." The logic for this was that, as parents, we would have to say no often enough without making it arbitrary or merely for our own convenience. If we said yes as often as we could, our no would carry more weight when it had to be used.

This was frightening to me. *Yes* is unknown. *Yes* can be disappointing. *Yes* pushes me out of my box. *Yes* is a risk.

But *yes* also releases the future. It releases hope. It releases dreams to be pursued. And the ultimate—it releases new life. When I said yes to Scott's proposal, a new life suddenly unfolded before me! Was it a risk? *Yes*. Love is always a risk. Was it unknown? *Yes*. Was it worth it? *YES!*

Now the Lord is calling each one of us to say yes. *Yes* to His invitation. *Yes* to His knock. *Yes* to letting Him in. *Yes* to dinner. *Yes* to life-change. *Yes* to setting up a home with Him.

The first dinner that Scott had with my family was a very big deal. My parents had already met him in a church setting, but now he was being invited into a more intimate family setting. That dinner was intended to communicate to him that we were accepting him at the next dimension. And I cooked my first food for him—Applesauce Oatmeal Muffins. (Those were intended to communicate that I was falling in love with him! I presume it worked since we wound up getting married!) Having a meal is more than just good eating, it is a place of
    Acceptance
      Communication
        Intimacy.

Intimacy with His people has always been God's goal. Throughout Scripture, we see this longing of God's presented over and over. We see it in the Garden of Eden when the Lord visited the first couple in "the cool of the day."[16] We see it in the Tabernacle, when He called His people to build so that He could meet, speak and dwell with them.[17] Many other Scriptures, too numerous to mention here, weave their way throughout the Old Testament, declaring God's desire to be ours, and for us to be His. But leap ahead to the New Testament where Jesus comes to dwell among us,[18] through to the end of the book of Revelation when the writer declares, "It's finally happened! The dwelling of God is with men!"[19] The desire of the ages, captured in a moment . . .

He wants to live with us.
>He wants a relationship with us.
>>He wants to eat with us.
>>>But we have to open the door.

If your beloved came to the door and knocked, you would open the door. You know you would! As surely as the bride in the Song of Songs declared, "My beloved put his hand by the latch of the door, and my heart yearned for him. . . . I arose to open for my beloved,"[20] you know that you would open the door to your bridegroom! Jesus—our Bridegroom—now stands at the door,

>Asking
>>Calling to you
>>>Will you say yes to the proposal?

Open the door . . . He wants to make a life with you!

---

1. See Isaiah 54:5.
2. Revelation 3:14-22, *NIV.*
3. "Laodicean Church," Wikipedia.org. http://en.wikipedia.org/wiki/Laodicean_Church#.22I_wish_that_you_were_cold_or_hot.22_.283:15.E2.80.9316.29, accessed June, 2011.
4. John 7:38.
5. Isaiah 44:3.
6. Psalm 46:4.
7. Revelation 22:17.
8. See Colossians 2:10.
9. See Genesis 2:24.
10. Hannah Hurnard, *Hinds Feet on High Places* (Portland, OR: ArType Services, 1972), p. 111.
11. See Ephesians 5:25-27.
12. See Romans 8:29.
13. See 2 Corinthians 3:18.
14. See Jeremiah 29:11.
15. See Hebrews 12:11.
16. Genesis 3:8.
17. See Exodus 25:8,22.
18. See John 1:14.
19. Revelation 21:3, author's paraphrase.
20. Song of Songs 5:4-5.

Encountering Him

TABLE MANNERS

Have you ever noticed that God is a good cook?

- He provided manna for Israel in the wilderness. The book of Hebrews describes it as "angel's food."
- Psalm 23 tells us that He prepares a table—a meal—for us, even in the most difficult of circumstances.
- Following His resurrection, Jesus prepared breakfast for His disciples on the beach (see John 21). Grilled bread and fish! That may not be your ideal morning meal, but breakfast on the beach sounds pretty nice to me!
- And Scripture ends with the marriage supper of the Lamb . . . to which we are all called.

Interestingly, many of Jesus' conflicts with the Pharisees were specifically over eating issues—when He ate, how He ate and with whom He ate. Jesus challenged the traditions that made eating just another religious exercise rather than an encounter with people. When you read through Scripture, look at all of the encounters Jesus had with people over food. He clearly enjoyed meals with friends!

I would like to invite you to have a meal with Jesus. We've already discussed that it is at the table, in the intimate home environment, that we experience acceptance, communication and intimacy. So, I repeat— I would like to invite you to have a meal—*a literal meal*—with Jesus.

One way you can do that is to celebrate Communion—the Lord's Table. Many of us celebrate that with regularity at church. But have you ever simply celebrated His Table with just Him? In my experience, there is nothing sweeter than celebrating Him and remembering all He has done for me on that kind of one-on-one basis.

There is nothing in Scripture that says a priest or pastor must administer the Lord's Table, but some might feel uncomfortable doing that by themselves. So, if you don't feel comfortable receiving Communion in this way, how about having a meal in His presence. (It could even be grilled bread and fish!) It can be breakfast, lunch or dinner, but eat it in His presence.

At our house, mealtime was the time we shared about our days and solved problems. Occasionally, it was a time to confront an attitude in a child or encourage someone regarding a difficulty. In this chapter, you read, "The Lord doesn't come into our lives to confront attitudes just for the fun of it. He is not arbitrary or haphazard. He always challenges us with the goal of bringing us to the full potential of what He has created us for." Ask Him if there is something He wants to do in your heart *today*. Ask Him for advice. Ask Him for words of encouragement. But in all . . . listen for His voice. Thank Him for all He has done in your life. Say yes to His proposal! He is knocking at the door, and He wants to come in and share a meal with you.

He brought me to the banqueting house, and his banner over me was love.
Sustain me with cakes of raisins, refresh me with apples, for I am lovesick.[1]

Give us this day our daily bread.[2]

So He humbled you, allowed you to hunger, and fed you with manna . . .
that He might make you know that man shall not live by bread alone;
but man lives by every word that proceeds from the mouth of the LORD.[3]

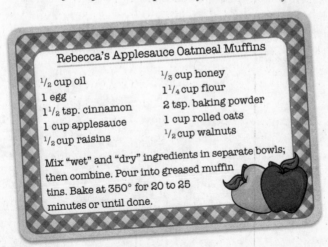

Rebecca's Applesauce Oatmeal Muffins

½ cup oil
1 egg
1½ tsp. cinnamon
1 cup applesauce
½ cup raisins

⅓ cup honey
1¼ cup flour
2 tsp. baking powder
1 cup rolled oats
½ cup walnuts

Mix "wet" and "dry" ingredients in separate bowls; then combine. Pour into greased muffin tins. Bake at 350° for 20 to 25 minutes or until done.

1. Song of Songs 2:4-5.
2. Matthew 6:11.
3. Deuteronomy 8:3.

THE DIAMOND

I recognized my engagement ring the minute I saw it!

Scott and I had begun talking about marriage. In fact, our very first discussion on the topic was a strange and awkward conversation. Who was going to be the first to say that we thought we were supposed to spend our lives together? Proposals don't come out of nowhere; there are things hinted at, questions asked, thoughts tossed around, responses measured. "What if . . . ?"

Then there comes a moment in every relationship when it is either going to end or move forward. To ignore that moment is to move the relationship into limbo; to move it forward requires that it be defined. We were at that point: We were going to break up or get married.

"What do you think is going to happen to us?" Scott asked.

"I don't know," I replied. (Brilliant comeback!) "What do you think?"

"I don't know."

Actually, we both knew; but that was our first conversation that began to broach the subject that this relationship may be permanent. Within a month we were looking at rings. And as I said, I recognized my engagement ring the minute I saw it. This shopping trip was our first foray to look at rings. Scott wanted to make sure that he got exactly what I liked, and so off we went to the jewelers.

And there it was.

It was literally the first ring I saw in the first store we walked into! Unfortunately for me, my groom-to-be didn't believe that any female could choose a ring that fast. He insisted that we keep looking . . . and looking . . . and looking. We spent the entire day going from jeweler to jeweler. I was exhausted; he was exhausted. We'd looked at more rings than I care to count. We'd learned all about the "four Cs"—color, cut, clarity and carat weight. Oh . . . and cost. I guess that would be the fifth C!

I think we went to a dozen different stores . . . and wound up back at the first store, purchasing the first ring we had seen!

A month later, he proposed in a beautiful location under a starry sky. Our moment.

Afterward, he had planned a dinner with all of our parents in attendance, at a lovely restaurant, with a fireside table, overlooking the beautiful city lights of Los Angeles. I was delighted, and spent the next weeks showing that ring off to anyone who would look. I admired my ring, cleaned it, had the prongs checked every other week. I wasn't taking any chances with that diamond!

Beyond its beauty, however, I loved what that ring stood for. In certain respects, a ring brings broadened definition. While a proposal may define the relationship between the couple, a ring defines it for all the world to see. Every time I looked at it, it reminded me of

> a promise
> > a covenant
> > > a love
> > > > a future.

These are the same things that should happen in our lives when we say yes to Jesus. Everything about how we are living should begin to change because we have His "ring on our finger." Everything in our lives should now be defined by Him.

I am giving you a white stone . . .

This was a lesson that the church at Pergamos had not learned. They had been deluded into believing that because they "no longer lived under the law" they could go do anything they wanted—including sin. Rather than being defined by Jesus, they were just adding Him in with everything else. Yes, they believed in Him. There was no mistaking that. But believing had not yet turned them into disciples—there were people in this church who were involved in idolatry and immorality.

While I can't guarantee that the white stone Jesus talks about here in Revelation is a diamond, it sounds a lot like it to me! He was offering the church at Pergamos an engagement ring . . .

and He's offering the same to us.

And to the angel of the church in Pergamos write, "These things says He who has the sharp two-edged sword: 'I know your works, and where you dwell, where Satan's throne is.

And you hold fast to My name, and did not deny My faith even in the days in which Antipas was My faithful martyr, who was killed among you, where Satan dwells. But I have a few things against you, because you have there those who hold the doctrine of Balaam, who taught Balak to put a stumbling block before the children of Israel, to eat things sacrificed to idols, and to commit sexual immorality. Thus you also have those who hold the doctrine of the Nicolaitans, which thing I hate. Repent, or else I will come to you quickly and will fight against them with the sword of My mouth. He who has an ear, let him hear what the Spirit says to the churches. To him who overcomes I will give some of the hidden manna to eat. And I will give him a white stone, and on the stone a new name written which no one knows except him who receives it.' "[1]

My son Brian seemed to take forever to propose. I'm sure it seemed even longer to his sweetheart, Melissa.

Brian and Melissa had become good friends in college, leading Bible studies together, studying together, chatting constantly. Many months into this friendship, they began dating—a good relationship with the solid foundation of friendship and the love of Jesus Christ. The next step was Brian bringing Melissa over to our house to visit with the family. She was there for dinners, parties, church events and just to hang out. We were getting to know her, and she was getting to know us.

And then the big one—extended family events! Melissa went to several family weddings and found herself mercilessly quizzed: "And when are the two of you going to have an announcement to make?" While that may be irritating to the family member, it's downright embarrassing to the non-family member. Melissa finally declared that she was not going to another big family event without a ring on her finger. While I agreed with her, her comment also let me know that though there had been no proposal or a ring yet, there was apparently an understanding.

But an understanding does not an engagement make!

As parents, we had yet to see Brian make a move in that direction. I remember at one point, Scott told him, "You'd better get a ring on

that girl's finger or you're gonna lose her!" (We tried not to be inter-
fering parents, but we also recognized the real deal when we saw her!)
Finally . . . a day was chosen,
      a question was asked,
            an answer was given,
                  and a ring was presented.

But up until that moment, Brian and Melissa were not "fully
engaged."

Fully Engaged

The church at Pergamos presents an interesting blend of faithfulness
and compromise. These people had stood strong in the face of persecution, but they countenanced sexual immorality. They lived in an
extremely pagan location—so intense that Jesus calls it "the place
where Satan dwells." Yet, they were involved in eating things sacrificed to idols—a key element in idol worship.

Faithfulness and compromise.

Most likely, the issues they faced grew out of a deeply flawed definition of our "freedom in Jesus Christ." There were those in Pergamos
who had bought into the lie that if they were free in Christ and *no
longer under the law,* they could pretty much do whatever they pleased.
Even commit sexual immorality. After all, they reasoned, didn't God
forgive everything? Isn't that what it meant to be free? The apostle
Paul addresses this in Romans when he says, "What shall we say then?
Shall we continue in sin that grace may abound? Certainly not!"[2]
Before we judge the Pergamenes too harshly, let's take an honest
look at ourselves. We not only live in a culture that could rightly be
termed "where Satan dwells," but we also face the same challenge of
not allowing our beliefs to influence every part of our lives. We say
that we believe in telling the truth, but we indulge in the occasional
"little white lie." We say that we believe in honoring the Lord with our
speech, but we think nothing of attending a movie filled with blas-
phemy. We steal that pen from the office. (*They've got lots more; they'll
never miss this. Besides, I worked overtime the other day . . . they owe me.*) We
bend the rules for ourselves. (*I know the Lord told me to go on a fast, but I
didn't know there was going to be this dinner. He'll understand, and I'll make*

it up on another day.) We say that we want to grow in Him, but we don't invest in the disciplines that make that possible. There are areas of our walk with Jesus where we're doing great and making obvious progress. Other areas maybe aren't so great.

It's in those areas that we aren't fully engaged.

We recognize "fully engaged" as an English idiom, and, like much of our language, it has multiple meanings. We might use it when we talk about gears meshing. The wheels are spinning, but you aren't going anywhere until the gears are fully engaged.

Medically speaking, "fully engaged" can refer to a baby who is now in position and ready to be born. Architecturally, it can refer to two building elements that are joined or linked together. The phrase can also be used of someone who is completely focused on what he is doing—"he is fully engaged in his work."

While we don't normally apply this phrase to people who are planning to be married, its uses can be profoundly descriptive of the process a couple walks toward marriage. There is something ready to be born . . . *new life*. There is something on which they are totally concentrating . . . *new focus*. There are two building elements (or in this case, two people) who have become completely linked . . . *new relationship*

new life
  new focus
    new relationship

In Pergamos, they had all of those definitions going on. Jesus commended them for standing firm and being faithful. They invested in life, even though persecution had brought death. They stayed focused on the Lord.

On the other hand, they had compromised in how they related to cultural and doctrinal issues. In other words, when the issues were black and white, they had no trouble recognizing what they were supposed to do. But when the issues at hand got blurred by "gray," they tended to drift off in the wrong direction.

The cultural issues they faced had to do with idols—very common in Pergamos. In fact, one of the major forms of idolatry was worship of the Roman emperor. Because idolatry was so infused into the culture, it was easy for it to become mixed in to daily life. You could hardly go anywhere without idolatry being right in your face.

Like TV . . . like music . . . like the Internet . . . like Facebook. Not that any of those things are inherently bad; but they are everywhere. They are hard to get away from. The temptations presented to us via our media can so easily get mixed in to our daily lives. Consider just a few things that can rule us.

- The housewife who gets her "high" by shopping for things she doesn't need.
- The teen who uses constant texting as a replacement for authentic relationships.
- The businessman who has to have the new model car every year.

These things seem so small compared to the immorality of Pergamos. We often look at things like shopping or texting or new cars as insignificant. The "big, bad sins" are the ones that really matter—stuff like substance abuse, pornography and murder. We wouldn't do *those* now, would we?

But even though we avoid the biggies, we let what we consider to be "lesser issues" slip by.

Yet those small things add up.

We make concession after concession, whispering sweet little lies to our conscience. Ultimately, we wind up living with blatant compromise instead of obvious, transparent, clear-hearted obedience.

If we only pay attention to the "big sins," and don't bring every thing before the Lord, we become like the church at Pergamos in the gray areas of life. There are many things that seek to rule our lives and demand our devotion. Materialism. Relationships. Politics and prestige. Finance and fashion. Anything can become an idol if it takes first place in your life. Even "good things" can become an idol. Second Kings 18:4 describes how the king of Israel destroyed the bronze serpent that Moses had made[3] because centuries later, the people were now *worshiping* it.

Amazing, isn't it? Something that at one time had been a means of salvation had become an idol.

It can slip in so easily while we are completely unaware. Before you know it, it has taken over. That's what happened to me with my computer. I had no idea how much that little machine ruled my days—until the Lord asked me to simply shut it down for one day a week. Twenty-four hours. No games. No email. No work. No Facebook. No pictures.

I was stunned to discover how all of that "silent noise" ran my life. Shocked to realize how difficult it was for me to simply turn the thing off. Amazed to finally realize how distracted I had actually become.

Maybe the Pergamenes weren't so unusual after all.

Perhaps the biggest surprise I found, though, was how easily I could hear His voice when I stopped letting something else run my life. On the days that I turn my computer off, the Lord always meets me; always gives direction for my life; always blesses me with His presence. In this one small way, I remind myself weekly that I am building a life with Jesus.

When we are engaged, everything is supposed to be defined by the beloved. In our relationship with the Bridegroom, we have to come to the point of deciding if we will allow ourselves to be defined by Him—in every area of our lives. Many people believe in Jesus. They have accepted salvation and will someday be with Him in heaven. But it's difficult to see life-change in them.

Jesus is just a secondary presence in their lives. Like a date. When you're dating, you can tell people, "I have someone in my life. I like spending time with that person! But I have my own life, too. Right?"

Accepting an engagement ring changes all of that. Not only is someone in your life, but he/she is there to stay! And that someone *will* change your life and define your future. In accepting the ring, you are accepting the potential of a new life in which everything will now be different.

Lord of the Ring

When you accept an engagement ring, you are giving the giver of the ring the right to define your life.

I will give you a white stone.

Accepting an engagement ring means that you're not going to date anyone else. It means that you're now putting all of your efforts

into building a life that involves the two of you. Decisions are now
made as a couple; you're not operating unilaterally anymore. Friends
may change as you step into a new life together. Activities change.

I called my brother-in-law one day, not long after he got married.
As he picked up the phone, he said, "Just a minute . . . I've got to take
the banana bread out of the oven."

Banana bread? I'd never known him to step into a kitchen except
to eat!

Activities and interests change. You are in the process of blending
two lives into one. You are now being defined by
        new life
            new focus
                new relationship

When we accept an engagement ring, we are accepting stewardship as well. Of course, we should steward the diamond. We shouldn't
treat it carelessly, leave it lying around or let our friends try it on. It's
a covenant gift from the beloved—not something to let the casual ob-
server try on or play with. We should take it to the jeweler's to be
checked so that we don't lose a stone.

We also steward it because it represents something greater that
we're also called to steward—a relationship.

Relationship. Covenant. Stewardship.

Stewarding a relationship requires time, intention, forgiveness
and laying down your rights. Engagement means we are setting aside
our rights as individuals in favor of serving what is best for *us*. We see
this beautifully lived out in the book of Ruth as she laid down every
right she had so that she could serve another:

> *Wherever you go, I will go;*
> *And wherever you lodge, I will lodge;*
> *Your people shall be my people,*
> *And your God, my God.*
> *Where you die, I will die,*
> *And there will I be buried.*
> *The LORD do so to me, and more also,*
> *If anything but death parts you and me.*[4]

This concept is completely foreign in our world today. A newly engaged woman once told me that her fiancé had accepted a job offer in another city. "Once we're married, do I have to move where he is? I just don't think that's fair."

That's the attitude of our day. Our world lives seeking what's "fair," evenhanded and politically correct. It has no concept of the sacrifice and service needed to nurture relationship. Self becomes the center of focus; self becomes the idol. Yet sacrifice and service are at the core of how we're called to live as followers of Jesus Christ, and in relationship with Him.

We sacrifice our most precious possessions—ourselves, our time.

We lay down our need to be right or get our own way.

We offer forgiveness when wronged—freely and without keeping score.

It's the way Jesus showed us how to live; it is the way He lives for us. He laid down His rights to provide forgiveness. The sacrifice and servanthood that He poured on us is now evidenced in His offer of

a white stone.

This isn't to say that being engaged is some kind of grim, constrictive existence. While you set aside the freedom to do some things (like date others or order your own life), you are at the same time accepting a different kind of freedom—freedom to trust, freedom to commit, freedom to share, freedom to put your life into the care of another. Freedom to love without reserve.

That kind of freedom will redefine your life.

Jesus calls us to trust Him that way. He calls us to lay down our "rights" and allow Him to define us, to be Lord of—*everything.*

Like many Christian parents, we gave each of our children a "covenant ring" or a "purity ring" when they reached the dating age of 16. If you've not heard of that concept before, it's a ring that signifies the commitment of the wearer to stay sexually pure—to live life God's way—until marriage.

When we gave Lindsey her ring, Scott and I took her out to a beautiful restaurant at the beach. Over dessert, Scott took out the ring that Lindsey had chosen as her covenant ring—a charming sapphire and diamond ring, appropriate for a 16-year-old. She already knew what it was supposed to stand for, but Scott reiterated it any-way. Then he concluded with a shocking statement. He said:

> I have always wanted my family to live honestly before each other. So I want us to be honest here. If you agree to accept this ring on the terms I just outlined, then you are agreeing that Mom and I will hold you accountable to that. But I won't have a daughter who talks a good Christian game and wears the ring on the outside, but is doing whatever she wants sexually. If you don't want to abide by what this ring represents, then let's be honest about it, and we'll go throw the ring in the ocean, and we'll know what to expect from you. But let's just be real honest right here and now.

Lindsey did accept the terms of the ring—not just from us but from the Lord. She was accepting a ring from us, but letting her life be defined by Jesus. She was choosing to live His way.

How about you? Have you accepted a white stone? Maybe you've already answered Jesus' proposal. Or maybe you just "have an under-standing" with Him. But until you have accepted the white stone that Jesus offers, along with all that it represents . . . you are not fully engaged.

Where Your Treasure Is

I remember my son Kyle going over his budget, trying to figure out how much he could spend on an engagement ring. Having gone over his figures, he went and talked to his dad. Scott encouraged him to spend a little more than he had planned. Scott was an economics ma-jor in college, so the advice to spend more was unusual.

"There are times in life," he told Kyle, "when you should spend *the most* you can. A time to do *everything* that you possibly can." Kyle, with the responsibilities of a soon-to-be-husband filling his vision, was try-ing to keep a financial buffer in savings. Wise move. But this was a time to do the most that he possibly could.

The ring becomes a symbol of what you're about to do: *give every-thing of your heart, your life, your body, your income, your endeavors, your care . . . to another.* Jesus said, "Where your treasure is, there your heart will be also."[5] When it comes to committing your heart to someone, it should show up in what you do with your "treasure."

I also once encountered a couple that had gotten married "on the spur of the moment." Apparently, they were on a date when they decided this was the moment to make the plunge. So, late at night, they drove around until they found a minister who would marry them. They didn't have rings . . . so they used a gum wrapper. At the time, everyone thought it was cute; but "cute" never makes up for investment, preparation and process. Sadly, over time, the lack of "putting your treasure where your heart is" also showed up.

There is a time to spend everything you possibly can.

Similarly, we can completely miss the point. A 20-something student, knowing that I had married off a couple of sons, cornered me with the question: "What if I want to marry someone and I have more money than her? I mean, then I'm investing more into the marriage than she is." He was obviously completely missing the point. It took a very long discussion to get his eyes off of the dollar amount.

Everything is . . . well, everything. And if you want a relationship to succeed, it will cost you everything.

Jesus did that for us. The Bible says that we have been given the riches of His grace.[6] Look at that again: "The riches of His grace!" Just think! The resources of heaven are at our disposal because He gave everything. *He spent the most that He could.* He became flesh. He gave His life. He has poured out His riches on us.

He gave everything, and now He asks for our everything in return. Though it may *feel* risky to us, it isn't. The Bible, talking about the coming of the Messiah, says that God lays, "A stone for a foundation, a tried stone, a precious cornerstone, a sure foundation."[7] That's a safe place for us to give everything.

Kyle found a beautiful ring for Teresa. And, yes—he spent the most that he could! The ring became a sign of where he had decided to invest his life.

Spending the most that you can also grows over time.

For our twenty-fifth anniversary, Scott decided that he wanted to replace the diamond in my engagement ring with a larger one; and he had figured out the perfect way to make it a surprise! The day that Brian was going to the jeweler's to pick up Melissa's engagement ring, Scott casually asked, "Have you had the prongs on your ring checked lately? No? Well, why don't we have Brian take it in and have it looked at?"

Pretty clever, huh?

Of course, Scott and the jeweler were in cahoots, and the jeweler immediately called me with a tale of how many repairs my ring needed! So on my twenty-fifth anniversary, I was given my ring . . . again . . . with a much larger diamond! I will never forget what Scott said to me:

> "I wanted to give this to you because our future is bigger than our past."

I have to admit that when he died just two short years later, I questioned that comment. I've learned to bring those things before the Lord, but I was angry. *If he was going to die, why did You let him say such a thing to me? My future isn't bigger . . . My future just ended.*

Gently, the Lord had to remind me: it's never a person who makes my future. It's Jesus, and Him alone. How like the Lord that is! When we say yes to Him, when we accept a new life, when we listen to His heart, when we receive His ring . . . our future will always be bigger than our past!

Rings have been an important part of my process of becoming someone new. There are now two times in my life that I've had to "become someone new"—once when I got engaged, and once when my husband passed away. When I got engaged, I began the process of going from Rebecca Hayford to Rebecca Bauer. It was a new identity . . . with new responsibility. And it was marked by the receiving of a ring.

Engagement rings are cause for great excitement! But do you see how Jesus takes us through a similar process?

New identity. New responsibility. I will give you a white stone . . .

When Scott died, I went through another season of becoming new. My name stayed the same, and I still wore my wedding ring for a long time. From the outside, I looked no different. Because of my circumstances, however, I was painfully aware of each step I took. I wore my diamond for quite a while, but eventually moved my rings to my other hand. Even later, I had the stone reset into another ring—not because I didn't still think it was beautiful as it was, but because God was (once again) making me into someone new, and leading me toward my future. Jesus met me in this season and I learned a new dimension of having my identity be in Him rather than in a person.

My heavenly Bridegroom, Jesus Christ, still calls to me. And He calls to you too.

Your future is bigger than your past!

Wherever you are in your life right now . . . living in expectancy (like a bride), or facing tremendous difficulty (like a widow), you are not excluded from receiving the white stone that Jesus offers. In Him, there is always a future.

Because He has conquered all of life and all of death, all of temptation and all of trial, He can stand before each one of us today and offer

Expectancy. A future. Hope. A promise. A white stone.

Accept it from Him today.

1. Revelation 2:12-17.
2. Romans 6:1-2.
3. See Numbers 21:4-8.
4. Ruth 1:16-17.
5. Matthew 6:21.
6. See Ephesians 2:7.
7. Isaiah 28:16.

Encountering Him

A WHITE STONE

Neil Armstrong once said, "Geologists have a saying—rocks remember." I love that quote, because I just love rocks! I haul them home from everywhere . . . the world's least expensive souvenir! In fact, Scott used to refuse to carry my suitcase because it was stuffed with rocks, shells, baggies filled with sand! In my office, I have a bowl filled with rocks from all over the world. I can actually put my hands on that bowl and touch the world. Or pray for the world. It's one of my favorite things!

I also have a rock on my front porch. I see it every day, and it reminds me of the commitment I have made to Jesus. In the book of Joshua, Israel was challenged, "Choose for yourselves this day whom you will serve."[1] When I placed that rock on my porch, it was intended to be a physical reminder of my commitment—to serve Jesus Christ; to acknowledge Him in all of my decisions; to live my life differently from the world. It reminds me that I have accepted His engagement ring and that I have given Him the right to order my life and be Lord of my life.

In Scripture, we see rocks used to commemorate victories and to set up memorials.[2] Stones, of course, are used in laying foundations. The Bible says that even our foundations will be laid with beautiful and costly stones.[3] "There is no rock like our God,"[4] the Bible declares. And altars abound throughout the Old Testament. Piles of stones were often placed at significant sites to remind the people of God's work in their lives. Further, Jesus said that if His people stopped praising, the rocks would begin to cry out in praise.[5] If rocks can praise, they can also remind.

When Jesus gives us "a white stone," it's to remind us that we are fully engaged to Him. May I encourage you to get a rock to commemorate your choosing Him? To remind you that you are living in an engagement period with Him? Start a bowl of rocks like I did, or set a bigger rock in your home or yard. Put it someplace where you will see it every day. You could get one of those paperweights that looks like a giant diamond, or find stone bookends or put a beautiful geode on your desk. You could even just get a rock out of your backyard and paint it white, as a reminder:

I am giving you a white stone.

Incredibly, Peter calls *us* living stones! Think about what that means: In a sense, we are the stones that represent Jesus' engagement—to us. As living stones, we proclaim to the world our choice of Him and His choice of us.

> *Come to the Lord Jesus, the "stone" that lives . . .*
> *The stone God chose, and he was precious.*
> *You also are like living stones,*
> *So let yourselves be used to build a spiritual temple—to be holy priests*
> *who offer spiritual sacrifices to God.*
> *He will accept those sacrifices through Jesus Christ.*[6]

Choosing
  Commemorating decisions
    Marking the "big moments" in your walk with Him!

> *Choose for yourselves this day whom you will serve . . .*
> *And he took a large stone, and set it up . . . [as] a witness.*[7]

---

1. Joshua 24:15.
2. See Joshua 4:1-24; 1 Samuel 7:12.
3. See 1 Kings 5:17; Isaiah 54:11.
4. 1 Samuel 2:2, author's paraphrase.
5. See Luke 19:40.
6. 1 Peter 2:4-5, *NCV*.
7. Joshua 24:15,26-27.

THE GOWN

Dresses. Dresses. Dresses.

When it comes to planning a wedding, there are a lot of dresses to think about! The bridal gown, of course, but there are also the bridesmaids' dresses—and of course, you'll be able to wear it again! Then there are the mothers' dresses, the flower girl dress and making sure that the guest book person, the greeters and the singers are all at least color-coordinated! (Lucky guys! You just step into a rented tux—and it's already chosen for you.) If you take a look at all of the wedding reality shows on TV right now, you clearly see that people can become obsessed with this topic!

Usually, the dress decisions fall into the territory of the bride. Lots of girls dream about their weddings while growing up—from playing with Barbie dolls, to poring over bride magazines, to getting up in the middle of the night to watch a royal wedding.

I did all of those things!

My cousin and I used to page through the magazines for hours together. I had a wedding idea for winter, spring, summer or fall. I planned my ideas out a thousand ways before I was out of junior high! And, of course, I was up for "the wedding of the century!" Charles and Diana. Never mind that I was already married and had two kids!

Knowing all of this, Scott and I created a phrase to remind our sons that there were decisions that should always be left to the bride. The phrase was: "The bride is always right." Intended only to remind two young men to occasionally "step away from the bride," we only had to use it a couple of times.

Mostly, with Kyle.

For some reason that still eludes me, Kyle decided he was going to leap into the bridesmaid dress discussion for his wedding. He had an opinion—and he wanted burgundy dresses for the girls.

Lovely color.

Except that Teresa wanted yellow.

One day, I was walking past his bedroom and heard him talking on the phone to her. I didn't know what they were saying because they were speaking in Spanish, but I could tell by Kyle's tone of voice that he was unhappy about something. Assuming that it was a wedding discussion, I poked my head into his room and whispered, "*The bride is always right!*" Later, I discovered that I was indeed correct. The discussion was over colors for the bridesmaids' dresses! And . . . the dresses were yellow.

Several weeks later, we were at church and I overheard Kyle rather intensely relating the dress color issue to one of his friends. As I walked by, I said to Kyle (again!), "Just remember . . . the bride is always right!"

Kyle's friend (who was also recently engaged) suddenly blanched and said, "If the bride is always right, I'm afraid to get married!"

"Oh, don't worry," I assured him. "The bride may always be right, but the *wife* isn't always right!"

The other young man heaved a sigh of relief, and we all had a good laugh. We also recognized the fact that brides have their wedding day to plan,

to celebrate,

to be the princess.

My daughter's wedding was the only one for which I was a working mom. When my sons were getting married, I was still in the stay-at-home-mom phase of my life. Then again, I was also only the mother of the groom for those two weddings, which dramatically changed my responsibilities.

The fact that suddenly I was working full time made some of the planning for Lindsey's wedding rather challenging. We would try to meet at lunch and run to look at something. We had lots of telephone consultations with vendors, and conversations with each other. Bride magazines marked with Post-its were all over the house so that we could each see what the other liked.

It was in this season that I discovered the beauty of the Internet and wedding websites.

One evening, Lindsey and I decided we would start looking at wedding gowns. It was late because she didn't get home from school until after 10 p.m. But we wound up on a website that showed literally *thousands* of gowns . . . and that evening we happily clicked our way through hundreds of them. It went something like this:

Click. A picture of a dress appears. Lindsey looks, says, "No," and—*click*—we move on.

There was *nothing* that she saw that evening that even came close to what she envisioned. Occasionally we would take a little longer to look at a dress as she explained parts of the design that she liked and parts that she didn't.

Click. "No." *Click. Click.* "No and no." *Click.*

For hours. Until we were both falling over with exhaustion and decided to go to sleep for the night.

At least by the end of the evening, I had a pretty good idea of what she was looking for.

The next morning, I was up and at it again. Being the Type A person that I am, I couldn't get this out of my mind, and a decision must be made! I started surfing around, looking for other websites, and came across one that had the word every mother of the bride longs to hear: *discount*.

What can it hurt? I asked myself.

They only had about 100 designs, but as I looked, I came across a gown that seemed to have everything Lindsey wanted . . . and it was beautiful!

"Lindsey, come in here and look at this dress!" I called.

She walked in, took one look at the dress and said, "Order it."

It was exactly what she had dreamed of.

....

The church at Sardis dreamed of a gown too. In fact, they had been promised one:

> *They shall walk with Me in white.*

But there were some issues that were potentially keeping them from receiving the promise. For the most part, they simply weren't ready for the Bridegroom to show up. They were unprepared.

In the letter to that church, Jesus pointed out that there were only a few who had "not defiled their garments." Throughout Scripture, clothing is often used to represent a person's moral and spiritual condition.[1] The Sardians wanted to receive their gown, but they weren't living as a "betrothed woman" should live. They had compromised—defiled their garments—and now were living on reputation, not reality.

The church at Sardis had a reputation for being "alive," but again Jesus challenges them: *You aren't what everyone thinks you are. I've promised you a white gown . . . but you're living a life that taints the purity of that gown.*

Traditionally, a white wedding gown was reserved only for a woman who had kept herself sexually pure. In today's world, regardless of lifestyle, the bride wears white. In fact, I recently came across a website that boasted a line of "maternity wedding gowns." The "reputation" of wearing a white gown is now considered obsolete and outdated. If you insist on white signifying purity, you'll be branded as both old-fashioned and judgmental.

It wasn't that way in the day Jesus wrote the letter to the church at Sardis. In fact, because He is the same yesterday, today and forever, the white gown (with accompanying lifestyle) is something He still insists on. Before you let the accuser begin to overwhelm you with condemnation, let me simply say that all of us have defiled our garments. If we tried to make them perfect on our own we would fail. None of us is adequate for that task.

Thankfully, Jesus not only insists on the white gown, but also He is committed to helping us possess it. The Bible says that He is committed to sanctifying and cleansing His Bride, with the washing of water by the Word, so that He can present her to Himself a glorious church without spot or wrinkle.[2]

You never need to ask if a promise in Scripture is for you. The Bible says that in Jesus Christ, every promise is yes and amen[3] to each one of us. So, regardless of what your past may have been, the promise to Sardis is for you too:

They shall walk with Me in white.

....

And to the angel of the church in Sardis write, "These things says He who has the seven Spirits of God and the seven stars: 'I know your works, that you have a name that you are alive, but you are dead. Be watchful, and strengthen the things which remain, that are ready to die, for I have not found your works perfect before God. Remember therefore how you have received and heard; hold fast and repent. Therefore if you will not watch, I will come upon you as a thief, and you will not know what hour I will come upon you. You have a few names even in Sardis who have not defiled their garments; and they shall walk with Me in white, for they are worthy. He who overcomes shall be clothed in white garments, and I will not blot out his name from the Book of Life; but I will confess his name before My Father and before His angels. He who has an ear, let him hear what the Spirit says to the churches.' "[4]

On the surface, the words to the church at Sardis are ominous; a second look, however, reveals a strong undercurrent of hope. Though the Sardians "are dead," not everything is dead: *Strengthen what remains.*

Though some have defiled their garments, not everyone has: *They shall walk with Me in white, for they are worthy.*

While Jesus tells them that He has not found their works perfect (literally "complete"), He calls them to: *Hold fast and watch.*

> *There is still time . . . still time to prepare the gown.*
> *Still time to get ready for the wedding.*

How Close Is Too Close?

In the book of Ruth, we read an account of how marriage intentions were processed in ancient Israel. Ruth approached Boaz and made her availability known by requesting, "Spread the corner of your garment over your maidservant."[5] The covering of the intended bride with the garment of the bridegroom was synonymous with engagement. Covering her with his garment showed intent to

> *bring under protection*
> *accept into the family*
> *redeem property*
> *provide economically*

Ruth needed all of those things.

When Ruth moved to Bethlehem with her mother-in-law, Naomi, both women arrived as widows. They were destitute, and without a male family member to redeem the ancestral land. We know the story . . . Ruth went into the fields during harvest to glean what she could. She was literally seeking provisions for Naomi and herself by picking up bits of grain that had been dropped by the hired harvesters. This was a long and grueling process, with little to show at the end of the day. Whatever she was able to scrape together was supposed to last them for the next year. Until the next harvest. As Ruth diligently worked, she wound up "harvesting" something else! She harvested redemption.

She met Boaz.

When Naomi heard Boaz' name, she realized this was a close enough relative that if a marriage could be arranged, the family property would be bought back. A memorial for the deceased would be secured. Protection for her and Ruth would become a reality. They would no longer be at the mercy of circumstance; they would be provided for. They would be redeemed.

The word used to describe this relationship is *ga'al.* The closest we can come to it in English is "kinsman-redeemer." The word is used throughout Scripture and means "to redeem, to act as a kinsman-redeemer, to avenge (by seeking justice), and to ransom." In other words, whatever you need—exacting justice, punishing enemies, buying back property, release from slavery, freedom from debt—the kinsman-redeemer—the *ga'al*—promises to take care of it.

This word is also used of God. Look at what Scripture reveals:

> *[He] redeems your life from destruction,*
> *[and] crowns you with lovingkindness.*[6]

> *He . . . redeemed them from the hand of the enemy.*[7]

> *For your Maker is your husband,*
> *The LORD of hosts is His name;*
> *And your Redeemer is the Holy One of Israel.*[8]

> *O Lord, You have pleaded the case for my soul;*
> *You have redeemed my life.*[9]

You get the picture. Boaz made this promise to Ruth when he extended
the corner of his garment over her; and Jesus makes the same kind of
promise to us.

> Redemption
> Freedom
> Provision
> Rest
> Security

We also see other examples of covering with the garment. Two places
in particular are of note. In Exodus 37:9, the same phrase that Ruth
used—*paras kanaph*—"stretch the corner of your garment over me," is
used. In Exodus, it is used to describe the cherubim that covered the
mercy seat on the Ark of the Covenant. They stretch their wings over
the seat of redemption. *Covering brings redemption.*

The Lord used similar language when He spoke to His people in
Ezekiel: "I spread My wing over you [*paras kanaph*] and covered your
nakedness. Yes, I swore an oath to you and entered into a covenant with
you, and you became Mine."[10]

> *Protection.*
> *Covenant.*
> *Covering.*
> *Belonging.*

A friend had this same type of experience at her wedding. She was
marrying a man of Scottish descent, and at one point in the ceremony,
he "covered her" with the family tartan—a very moving moment of covenant and acceptance.

But I have a question . . .

> *How close do you have to be
> for someone to cover you with his garment?*

My guess is . . . pretty close. My guess is also that the mere proximity of that person to you can challenge your comfort zone and invade
your personal space. But that is Jesus' intent; His proximity is intended
to move us out of our comfort zone and challenge us to change.

Isaiah experienced this. He was in the Temple of the Lord, and he
saw a vision where "the train of His robe filled the Temple."[11]

But we're the Temple now. Paul writes:

Do you not know that your body is the temple of the Holy Spirit
who is in you, whom you have from God,
and you are not your own?[12]

. . . you became Mine.

If the train of His robe is going to fill us, to cover us, not only are marriage intentions being made known, but also you have to be pretty close to the Bridegroom for that to take place.

How close are you to Jesus?
Are you close enough for the train of His robe to cover you?

Isaiah's vision went even further. Not only was he covered with the garment of the Lord, but also the vision made him immediately aware of his own uncleanness and unpreparedness. Isaiah would later write that our own righteousness is nothing more than filthy rags.[13] But we have hope—like Ruth. We have a promise—like the Sardians. When we come to Jesus and ask Him to stretch the corner of His garment over us, we trade in our own garments and receive the garments of righteousness. We, in fact, become clothed with Christ.

Covered.

Accepted.

Cleansed.

Redeemed.

They will walk with Me in white.

Ready or Not!

Isaiah knew all too well how incomplete he was when standing in the presence of the Almighty. Sadly, we often breeze through life thinking we're "doing pretty well." We think we're ready. This is how the Sardians were thinking. Jesus challenged them to "be watchful," and "strengthen what remains," because "your works aren't complete."

Much of the wealth of Sardis was based on the textile industry. They produced wool, and they were famous for the beautiful dyed cloth that they fashioned. Perhaps the Sardians had become confident in their own ability to create a beautiful gown, and had become less interested in the gown that Jesus offered. Whatever the issue was, the fact remained that they weren't as ready as they thought they were.

I remember when the flower girl from my wedding (who was three at the time) became a bride herself. Just as she was about to walk down the aisle, the wedding planner "fluffed" the skirt of her dress so that it would hang perfectly around her. It must have been quite a fluff, because the front flew up and brushed against her face . . . and left lipstick on the front of the skirt.

The musicians were signaled to keep playing for a few minutes while they tried to get the stain out. They rubbed, they tried the soap in the ladies room, they tried everything they could find; but nothing was working. The lip-prints remained. Someone finally brought in some liquid paper from one of the church offices, and they simply had to cover the stain. Thankfully, the dress was a brilliant white, so the fluid worked. But what a heartbreaking occasion for any bride . . .

to arrive at "the moment" and suddenly find out
you weren't ready after all.

Jesus talked about a situation like this. He told a story about some women who found themselves unprepared when the bridegroom arrived.[14] He described "ten virgins" who were awaiting the wedding. In our culture, we would describe these young women more like bridesmaids. In the wedding traditions of ancient Israel, these young women would have also been awaiting the bridegroom so that they could assist and escort the bride.

As they waited, five of them were fully prepared—knowing that the bridegroom could come at any hour of the day or night. In fact, culturally, that was part of the fun—the bridegroom surprising the ardent and hopeful bride! The five knew their responsibility, and they had their lamps by their beds, filled with oil and ready to go. The other five did not prepare. Who knows why? Maybe it was late. Maybe they had other things to do. They had their lamps, but they weren't full of oil. The bridegroom had already delayed . . . what was one more night? But it turned out to be *the* night. And

they weren't ready.

It's the way my family was for the 1994 Northridge (California) earthquake. The weekend before the earthquake, Lindsey, who was nine at the time, was supposed to be cleaning her room, but she got distracted by the flashlight that I required everyone to keep by his (or her) bed. We live in an earthquake-prone area, so I thought everyone having a flashlight nearby was a good idea.

Lindsey pulled hers out and turned it on. Sure enough, the batteries had run out. So she brought it to me asking if I would put in new batteries. I felt frustration because *she was supposed to be cleaning her room*. But what I viewed as a delaying tactic, turned out to be provision for our family less than 48 hours later. When the earthquake hit at 4:30 A.M., we all pulled out our flashlights . . . and Lindsey's was the only one that worked. As we crawled across floors littered with broken glass in a house that was rocking back and forth, guided only by Lindsey's flashlight, I realized: She had gotten ready; and I had not heeded a warning.

When the bridegroom showed up, Scripture says that "those who were ready went in with him to the wedding."[15] The five who were unprepared were gone when he arrived; they were out trying to buy oil in the middle of the night. When they finally arrived at the wedding, they were too late, and the door was closed.

The moment had passed, and they missed it.

Unprepared.

Alone.

Denied entrance.

Caught in the dark.

Jesus ends the parable by saying, "Watch . . ." Be prepared; have everything in readiness. Paul echoes this: "Watch, stand fast in the faith, be brave, be strong."[16] And now again, in the letter to Sardis, the reminder goes out, "be watchful."

Sardis had a history of not being watchful. As a city, they had grown over-confident in their own ability to take care of themselves. Sardis is set up on a hill that has cliffs on three sides that are so steep that the Sardians presumed they were safe. They only guarded what they knew was weak—the one side of the hill that had obvious entrance to the city. Because of their lack of watchfulness, they had been conquered not once . . . but twice!

Now Jesus points to their past and implores them not to repeat it:

Be watchful!
Guard what's weak; guard what's strong.
Strengthen what remains.
Hold Fast! Overcome!

And walk before Me in white.

When we talk about being close, like Isaiah; or being ready, like the Sardians; or having their lamps filled, like the virgins in the parable—we can too easily set it all aside as "just being about the return of Jesus Christ." Like Sardis, we are tempted to live like we have plenty of time to finish getting ready. We opt for comfort, and we stop being watchful. We become lax, like the unprepared virgins in Jesus' story; we don't think we need to be ready *today*.

We think of our life in the Lord as "event oriented" and "today" becomes less urgent. When Scott and I got engaged, he didn't propose and then disappear. While we were engaged, I heard from him every day. It wasn't just "events": proposal . . . wedding . . . honeymoon . . . *and they lived happily ever after.* And with the Lord, it isn't just salvation . . . marriage supper . . . eternity . . . *and they lived happily ever after.*

Jesus wants to "come to us" every day. It may not be "the wedding day" yet, but He still wants to talk to us, see us, know us. He's still at work in our lives. Are you allowing Him to get close? Close enough to cover you with His garment? Close enough to move you out of Sardian-like complacency? Are you watching and getting ready so that you are a Bride without spot or wrinkle? It is only until the fire of God touches our lips . . . enters us to purify and cleanse . . . that we can be made ready. But we have to watch for His coming and allow Him entrance.

Say Yes to the Dress

Jesus told another parable about a wedding. In this story, a king had invited friends to the marriage of his son. When the day arrived for the wedding, all of the guests had excuses why they couldn't come. Some of them were even good excuses. But it didn't change the fact that a royal wedding was about to take place and there wasn't going to be anyone to celebrate the big event!

So the king sent his servants into the city to invite any and all who would come. Even the poorest of the poor were invited. In the culture of the day, it wouldn't have been unusual for the king to provide the guests with appropriate attire; so as they arrived, they were each provided with a garment suitable for the occasion. It must have been a beautiful sight!

Except for one person. The parable doesn't tell us anything regarding the social or financial status of this individual . . . except that his lack of a wedding garment clearly stood out. The king was irate! This person was a blot on an otherwise perfect event.

Why would someone refuse the provision of a king? When you think about it, there are only a couple of reasons to refuse, and they reveal heart attitudes to which we are all susceptible:

- He could simply have not liked what the king had provided. "It's not my style"—asserting an independence that put the focus on him instead of on the covenant event and the principle players.
- He could have pridefully thought, *The way I am is good enough. Why should I have to change for this?*
- Maybe he didn't respect the king. This man may have just shown up because it was a free meal—he was in it for what he could get, but he had no love for the king himself.

We can't even imagine having the wedding garments provided for us—especially since we're the Bride. Brides spend a lot of time finding The Dress—the gown that expresses their style, or is how they want to appear before their groom. But our gown has been provided by the Bridegroom Himself. Whether we think that is acceptable or not, we have to challenge the attitudes in our own hearts that make it "all about us." Accepting a gown provided by the Bridegroom requires

Humility. Thanksgiving. Contentment. Acceptance.

Ezekiel movingly, and in great detail, describes God's provision of garments for His Beloved:

"I spread My wing over you and covered your nakedness. Yes, I swore an oath to you and entered into a covenant with you, and you became Mine," says the Lord GOD. "Then I washed you in water; yes, I thoroughly washed off your blood, and I anointed you with oil. I clothed you in embroidered cloth and gave you sandals of badger skin; I clothed you with fine linen and covered you with silk. I adorned you with ornaments, put bracelets on your wrists, and a chain on your neck. And I put a jewel in your nose, earrings in your ears, and a beautiful crown on your head. Thus you were adorned with gold and silver, and your clothing was of fine linen, silk, and embroidered cloth. You ate pastry of fine flour, honey, and oil. You were exceedingly beautiful, and succeeded to royalty. Your fame went out among the nations because of your beauty, for it was perfect through My splendor which I had bestowed on you."[17]

Jesus, in His kindness and grace, accepts us as we are, but He also provides robes for us that are much grander than we could have provided for ourselves. So what does that gown look like? It's beautiful!

> *For as many of you as were baptized into Christ*
> *have put on Christ.*[18]

Clothed in Glory.
    Robes of righteousness.
        Raiment of needlework.[19]

> *He has clothed me with the garments of salvation,*
> *He has covered me with the robe of righteousness,*
> *As a bridegroom decks himself with ornaments,*
> *And as a bride adorns herself with her jewels.*[20]

....

For my daughter's wedding, my dress was chosen by someone else. And the search for it was quite an event! I mean, when you're the mother of the bride, you *really* don't want to look like you're old enough to be marrying off a daughter, and I simply couldn't find anything I liked.

So again, on lunch hours, Lindsey and I would run up to the mall or to other stores near where we worked. We surfed the Web and perused magazines. In a more desperate moment, I think I even went to the fabric store and looked at patterns.

The search yielded nothing.

We started coordinating calendars to go downtown to the garment district on a Saturday, but as it turned out, we didn't have to go. On one of our lunchtime forays we came across the most beautiful "MOB" (Mother of the Bride) dress I had ever seen. Beautiful beaded skirt . . . jacket with rhinestone buttons . . . silk charmeuse blouse.

It was perfect . . . except that it was white.

Or so barely off-white that you really couldn't tell the difference from a distance. I loved it; Lindsey loved it. But how can you have a wedding where more than one person is wearing white?

"This is the perfect dress, Mom. Get it!"

"I can't wear this . . . only the bride is supposed to wear white."

"You can wear white if the bride tells you to . . . *the bride is always right!*"

The day of the wedding, we both had our hair done; we both had our makeup done; we both wore our white dresses. And we both looked beautiful!

How can you have a wedding where more than one person is wearing white? The marriage supper of the Lamb . . . and Jesus whispers to us, His beloved,

O my love, you are as beautiful as Tirzah,
Lovely as Jerusalem,
Awesome as an army with banners![21]

You are all fair, my love,
And there is no spot in you.[22]

1. David Aune, *Word Biblical Commentary,* vol. 52A (Dallas, TX: Word Books, 1997), p. 222.
2. See Ephesians 5:26-27.
3. See 2 Corinthians 1:20.
4. Revelation 3:1-6.
5. Ruth 3:9.
6. Psalm 103:4.
7. Psalm 106:10.
8. Isaiah 54:5.
9. Lamentations 3:58.
10. Ezekiel 16:8.
11. Isaiah 6:1.
12. 1 Corinthians 6:19.
13. See Isaiah 64:6.
14. See Matthew 25:1-13.
15. Matthew 25:10.
16. 1 Corinthians 16:13.
17. Ezekiel 16:8-14.
18. Galatians 3:27.
19. See Psalm 45:14.
20. Isaiah 61:10.
21. Song of Songs 6:4.
22. Song of Songs 4:7.

Encountering Him

WHAT WILL YOU WEAR?

Like preparing for a wedding, every detail counted when I was getting ready for a date. Whenever I was going to meet my beloved, I wanted to look perfect! My outfit, my hair, the jewelry, shoes, nail polish, brows plucked, legs shaved, perfume on! It all mattered.

I've thought about that idea when I've gone to church too. After all, I am planning to meet my Beloved—Jesus—there.

Recent years have seen a general tendency to "dress down" for church. I know that Jesus loves us as we are; I know that it isn't about how we look; I know that there are people who focus so much on what they're wearing that it becomes all about them. But I would never have gotten ready for a date that way.

Clothing can also show respect. When my son Kyle was eight years old, my brother-in-law was killed in a military accident. As we were getting ready for the funeral, Kyle walked out of his room, wearing a windbreaker instead of his blazer. I was upset and sent him back to change, with a few words about showing respect. However, I'd been so focused on what he "wasn't wearing" that I didn't notice the details. Before he went back to his room to change, Kyle stood quietly for a moment, and then said, "I thought this would be showing respect because I have all of Uncle Tom's squadron patches on this jacket."

What had initially looked disrespectful to me wasn't at all. Kyle had thought about it and worn the squadron patches jacket with respect.

Of course, that is only talking about clothes. How we present ourselves to Jesus will ultimately always still come down to a matter of heart.

The Bible has a surprising amount to say about how we "dress ourselves." Scripture says that we can actually clothe ourselves with violence,[1] cursing[2] or pride.[3] Have you ever headed out to church dreading the possibility of running into someone? Maybe you've allowed yourself to be clothed with unforgiveness or bitterness or lack of courage to resolve an issue. Scripture advises us that if we have anything against a brother or sister, we *must* take care of it before we come to worship.

If you bring your gift to the altar, and there remember that your brother
has something against you, leave your gift there before the altar, and go your way.
First be reconciled to your brother, and then come and offer your gift.[4]

This isn't the moment to cast blame or even to rehash whatever happened. *That* may need to be done with a trusted third party. A lady once came up to me at church and said, "I want you to know that I forgive you." Honestly, I had no idea that I had done anything to offend! But a statement like that immediately puts the other person on the defensive; it isn't going to settle anything.

However, it may be the time to simply go to the brother or sister and say, "I love you, but I know that I've wounded you. How can we resolve this?"

What if this Sunday, you dress to meet the Beloved? We get a choice of what we will wear. Besides the "clothing" listed above, Scripture also tells us that we can be clothed with joy, praise,[5] salvation, strength and honor.[6] As you prepare for church this Sunday, allow the Lord to prepare you inwardly and outwardly.

You have created me . . .
and have woven me together in my mother's womb.
Marvelous are Your works . . .
Everything that makes me—my frame, my might, my strength—
was not hidden from You, when I was made in secret,
And You skillfully wove me together . . .
So examine and investigate me, O God,
and be intimately acquainted with my heart, my soul, my mind—
I open all to You;
Test and prove me, be intimately acquainted with my anxieties;
And see if there is any sorrow, or sin, or idol
That has become a way of life in me,
And lead me in the path of eternity.[7]

---

1. See Psalm 73:6.
2. See Psalm 109:18.
3. See 1 Peter 5:5. (Peter equates our ability to submit with humility; submission actually winds up being a tool that resists pride in our lives!)
4. Matthew 5:23-24.
5. See Isaiah 61:3.
6. See Proverbs 31:25.
7. Psalm 139:13-15,23-24, excerpted and paraphrased by looking up the Hebrew words in *Strong's Concordance* and BlueLetterBible.org.

rebecca hayford bauer · www.regalbooks.com

THE NAME

When I got married at 19, I still went by the name "Becki." Even back then, "Becki Bauer" seemed just a little too cutesy. But when you're a teenager, you can get away with it.

As I matured, I wanted to be called "Rebecca," even though I'd never been called that before. It felt unnatural and strange. If someone actually used it, calling me from across the room, I felt like I was in trouble for something.

Scott tried every derivation of my name—Reba, Becca, Becker. He even threw in a few of his own: Rebecki, and Ree-beck. (I *hope* those were jokes!) None of them worked for me. But regardless of how funny it felt, the Becki/Rebecca debate was on.

Several times, at what seemed like obvious transition points, Scott would ask if I wanted to make the leap and switch to Rebecca. One time in particular, we moved to a new town to pastor, and no one knew us there. He figured that if I was really serious about this, it would be the perfect opportunity. He was right. But I still backed away from actually making the big switch. As much as I liked the name, it just didn't seem . . . familiar. And so the debate continued. For years.

Finally, in exasperation one day, Scott said, "Why don't you ask Jesus what *He* calls you?"

Excellent idea.

And so I did. The Lord answered me several days later, and what He said completely surprised me:

"I call you 'Scott Bauer' . . . because you're one with him." Becki or Rebecca wound up not mattering so much after all. The bigger issue was Relationship. Unity. Covenant.

And God called me "Scott Bauer."

In our independent, politically correct culture, this could offend some. It definitely goes against the grain of contemporary thought.

To some, of course, it isn't acceptable to take the husband's name at all. Americans, in particular, place a very high value on independence. (We even wrote a declaration about it and fought a war over it to establish our nation.) Actually, I have no argument with any woman who chooses to retain her maiden name. The reasons people do this are countless.

What matters, of course, is motive. The heart behind the action. And that is between the woman and her Lord. I have seen women retain their name for both positive and negative reasons.

Yes, it would concern me if a Christian woman made such a decision in order to cling to her old identity or assert her independence. Frankly, Jesus will challenge those attitudes in us anyway—whether we're male or female—at every turn. The lessons that we learn in Christ will always be spiritual at their root, will call us to complete dependence on Him and will ultimately find their greatest fulfillment in Him. Those lessons will also always come back to the heart, and that's what God is looking at. "For the LORD does not see as man sees; for man looks at the outward appearance, but the LORD looks at the heart."[1]

To really understand the relationship, unity and covenant that God wants to bring to a marriage, we need to take a look at the very first couple. God's intent for them was complete unity in everything: dominion, rulership, partnership, family, worship and obedience.

And name.

While I'm not about to make a doctrine out of this, I find it remarkable that as Scripture unfolds the story of humankind's beginning, the woman did not receive a separate name until after sin had entered the picture. The closest we can come to names for them is when Adam (literally "humankind") says, "She shall be called Woman, because she was taken out of Man."[2] They were "Adam the Man," and "Adam the Woman." When God calls "Adam" after they had eaten the fruit, He was calling both of them.[3]

Where are you?

Created for unity, created for oneness, the Man and Woman shared equally in everything.

Until sin.

Sin changed it all.

Immediately, shame enters the picture as they slink into the shrubbery to piece together an outfit to meet the Almighty in. When He shows up, shame quickly shifts to blame as the Man points his finger not only at the Woman but also at God Himself! *The woman You gave me*[4]—she's the problem.

Adam basically throws his wife under the bus. Quite the opposite of what we see "the last Adam,"[5] Jesus Christ, do for His bride: Christ loved the Church and gave Himself for her.[6] The Bible says that Adam received life, Jesus gives life; Adam betrayed his wife, Jesus laid down His life for His Bride.

But on that dreadful day, division was set in motion, competition was instigated, blame was cast, and punishment was pronounced. It was in this environment that the Man gave the Woman another name: Eve. The mother of all living. "Here's what you're good for now, Eve. Produce children."

But before that, their name was shared, implying

Unity.

Agreement.

Harmony.

One accord.

In Christ, the Lord always seeks to bring couples back to the unity He originally intended them to share. Peter calls it "heirs together."[7] It's also what Jesus wants. He longs for total unity. With you.

Heirs Together.

And it starts with a name.

The church in Philadelphia knew all about names. In fact, their city name had been changed before. Following the earthquake of AD 17, the emperor Tiberius assisted the city's recovery by granting a five-year tax relief. (Wouldn't *that* be nice.) They expressed their gratitude by renaming the city in his honor—Neocaesarea. New Caesar. But they eventually reverted back to Philadelphia.

Decades later, they renamed the city in honor of the emperor Vespasian. Again—the city eventually returned to its original name. Philadelphia. Names are all about definition, and the Philadelphians used the changing of their city's name to define who they honored, to convey thanks and to show their loyalty to their patron and ruler.

Now, Jesus—the Lamb who is worthy to receive

power and riches

wisdom and strength

honor and glory and blessing[8]—

is talking to them about a new name. In fact, He talks to them about several names that He wants to write on them: His name, His city's name and a new name.

Jesus is about to redefine their world!

....

And to the angel of the church in Philadelphia write, "These things says He who is holy, He who is true, 'He who has the key of David, He who opens and no one shuts, and shuts and no one opens: "I know your works. See, I have set before you an open door, and no one can shut it; for you have a little strength, have kept My word, and have not denied My name. Indeed I will make those of the synagogue of Satan, who say they are Jews and are not, but lie—indeed I will make them come and worship before your feet, and to know that I have loved you. Because you have kept My command to persevere, I also will keep you from the hour of trial which shall come upon the whole world, to test those who dwell on the earth. Behold, I am coming quickly! Hold fast what you have, that no one may take your crown. He who overcomes, I will make him a pillar in the temple of My God, and he shall go out no more. I will write on him the name of My God and the name of the city of My God, the New Jerusalem, which comes down out of heaven from My God. And I will write on him My new name. 'He who has an ear, let him hear what the Spirit says to the churches.' " ' "[9]

His Name, Her Name

Being redefined by names is not unusual when you think about being engaged and getting married. At weddings, names change. Titles change. Roles change. Mr. and Mrs.; husband and wife.

But the name of the beloved still burns in your heart. When you're in love, you just can't seem to get enough of his or her name! When I was dating Scott, I looked for reasons to say his name. I was ready to sing the wonders of Scott Bauer to anyone who was willing to listen! *Sigh!* What a guy! Sometimes I would even just say his name to myself because I wanted to hear it. And my Bible college notes have Scott's name doodled all around the edges. Hearing his name, saying his name, filled my heart with joy.

I'm my beloved's and He is mine.

It leads me to wonder . . . what do you call Jesus?

We often use titles for Jesus—Savior, Lord, King. Or, we use names that define things He does—advocate, shepherd, truth. But I've recently noticed a trend among believers of referring to Jesus only as "God" or "Christ," and not by His name. Not that any of those titles are wrong; they're all true. But they aren't *His name*. Scripture tells us that there is power and salvation inherent in the name of Jesus.

You shall call His name JESUS,
for He will save His people from their sins.[10]

God also has highly exalted Him
And given Him the name which is above every name,
that at the name of Jesus every knee should bow . . .
and that every tongue should confess that Jesus Christ is Lord.[11]

There is no other name under heaven given among men
by which we must be saved.[12]

Salvation is provided in His name. Authority is given in His name. And the Bible says there is *no other name* that does that! We need to be bold to use His name. In the book of Acts, as soon as the Church is released into the world, we see that in the name of Jesus the sick are healed, signs and wonders demonstrated, the good news proclaimed and captives freed.[13] When we pray "in Jesus' name," we are both accepting and entering into all that He, as our Bridegroom, came to provide for us. The Bible says that His name is as ointment poured forth.[14]

So . . . what do you call Him? He wants to hear His name from your lips.

Jesus

He loves your name, too, you know. As much as He wants to hear you say His name, He whispers yours. Have you ever heard Him call to you? When you hear Him call . . . there is only one response. "Here I am." *I'm right here, Lord.*

Kyle and Teresa speak only Spanish in their home, and there's one word that I have come to love: *mande*. When one calls the other, the response is "mande." *I'm yours to command.*

When Jesus drew you to salvation, how did He call you? How did He woo your heart? What are the circumstances that brought you? When did He first say your name to you? And what did you say back?

Here I am. I'm Yours to command. Mande.

"I will take up the cup of salvation," our hearts cry to Him, "and call upon the name of the LORD."[15] His sweet response, "Because he has set his love upon Me, therefore I will deliver him; I will set him on high, because he has known My name."[16] He not only wants to hear His name from your lips, but He also longs to put on you the intimacy and the unity of a name. His name.

Set me as a seal upon your heart.[17]

Thus says the LORD, who created you . . . and He who formed you . . .
"Fear not, for I have redeemed you;
I have called you by your name; You are Mine."[18]

What's in a Name?

We received an amazing array of gifts for our wedding. There were things we really needed right away: dishes, pots, pans, towels. There were some unique handmade gifts: an afghan made by my great-gramma, and some hand-thrown pottery. We got married in 1976—so we got some commemorative bicentennial gifts too: a pie server with a Fourth of July motif, and a George Washington paperweight. Then, there were duplicates—we received *five* crockpots.

And there were some funny gifts—a cookie jar that looked like a hut with gnomes around it, and a triangular-shaped metal serving plate that looked like we could attach it to a pole and use it as a spear point.

This was in the pre-wedding registry days, and all gift selections were up for grabs. When registries began, I remember some people being upset that it was as though the bride and groom were telling you what to get for them. Well—if you would like to give the duplicate or the funny gift, you can still do that. But wedding registries actually allow everything to match! (I like "matching.")

One of the presents we were given was a letter "B." I happened to be the one who opened that gift, and as I pulled it out, I said, "Cool! This is really neat! *B* for Becki . . . where's the *S* for Scott?"

Scott looked at me incredulously and said, "I think the *B* is for Bauer."

Oops . . . I hadn't gotten used to my new name yet! Getting used to a new name takes a bit of time. I think it took about a year before writing Bauer as my last name felt natural.

Jesus promises the church in Philadelphia that He will give them a new name. That's an exciting prospect, because in Scripture, names were given for more reasons than we typically give them now. Often they showed character traits. For example, "Nehemiah" means "Yahweh comforts." World events also inspired the names of children. We read about a baby who was named Peleg (divided), "for in his days the earth was divided."[19]

But more importantly, names can carry prophetic significance. Look at Abram's name change to Abraham as he receives the promises of God: "No longer shall your name be called Abram [exalted father], but your name shall be Abraham [father of a multitude]; for I have made you a father of many nations."[20]

The giving of a new name in biblical tradition ordinarily meant a change in the character, conduct or status of an individual.[21] Jacob went from being a "cheater" to being a "prince with God."[22] Joseph's change of status came when Pharaoh gave him an Egyptian name.[23] Jesus called James and John "the sons of thunder," and He told Peter that he would become rock-solid.[24]

Names, and new names, are a big deal in Scripture!

Knowing this, Scott and I were very intentional with the names of each of our children. We prayed long and hard, looked up definitions and asked the Lord to give us names for our children that would speak prophetic significance and identity into their lives.

Despite that intentionality, we faced the same angst that most parents face in choosing a name, and at the moment Lindsey was born, Scott and I had not yet agreed on a name. This was before the sonogram age, and we didn't know the gender of our baby until she was born.

When the doctor announced, "It's a girl!" we were elated! Though we would have been happy either way, after two boys, it was nice to have "some of each." But we hadn't agreed on a name. I was lying there exhausted, and thinking, *Please don't ask her name . . . please don't ask her name.*

Of course, the doctor immediately asked, "What are you going to name her?" Scott looked at me and said, "Well?" No pressure. Ask the exhausted woman who's just given birth to make the final decision!

We wound up using the first name I wanted and the middle name Scott wanted: *Lindsey Catherine.* Beautiful name.

And she received her identity.

But I want to talk about other names that also seek to give us identity—names that are neither appropriate nor beautiful. These are names that whisper in your mind . . . stupid, fat, incompetent, liar. Sometimes those names are phrases: "You'll never amount to anything." "You think you're good at *that*?!" "It's too bad you aren't as cute (or thin, or talented, or . . .) as your cousin." There are even family names: alcoholic, divorced, failure. These are names that whisper to us, no matter how old we get. "Can't you do anything right?" "You never were any good at math."

All of us have those kinds of names somewhere in our background. And Jesus steps into the picture and promises

I'll write on him a new name.

The Bible talks about a man who asked for a new name: Jabez. Jabez' story is related in a two-verse section of Scripture, and most of us would never have heard of him if it weren't for Bruce Wilkinson's brilliant book *The Prayer of Jabez.*

But Jabez wanted a new name.

"Jabez" literally means "pain." The Bible says that "his mother called his name Jabez, saying, 'Because I bore him in pain.'"[25] That must have been some delivery. This also meant that his entire life, every time anyone called him, it was prefaced with, "Hey, Pain . . ."

> Pain, dinner's ready.
> Time to go to bed, Pain.
> Could you check on the goats, Pain?

At some point, Jabez decided enough was enough. He called on the Lord and asked Him to keep him from causing pain. He didn't change his literal name, but he wanted the outflow of his life to be different. One of the sweetest verses in Scripture says, "So God granted him what he requested."[26]

This illustrates an amazing opportunity that each of us is offered, especially in light of the Lord's promise to the Philadelphians. Whatever name has been given to you that holds you back, the Lord offers a new name. Come as simply as Jabez and ask the Lord to change that name.

> *You shall be called by a new name,*
> *which the mouth of the LORD will name.*[27]

There's a Place for Us

Once I got used to my new name, I put it everywhere I could think of! I had the letter *B* on the front of the house. Someone gave us a stone with "Bauer" engraved into it. Door knockers, scrapbooks, CD holders, luggage—I was proud of my new name. It was a sign of belonging, a sign of my family, a sign of what Scott and I were building. It was a sign of *us.* The Bauer House was easy to identify!

The fact is, places and names go together. The prophet Isaiah speaks of that concept when he writes, "To them I will give in My house and within My walls a place and a name.[28] The place of our dwelling, and the name of our family: a place and a name. This was part of the promise to the Philadelphians too:

I will write . . . the name of the city of My God,
the New Jerusalem, which comes down out of heaven . . .

The Lord has had a love affair with "the city of God" throughout the centuries. When God talks about His love for His city, He speaks in the most passionate of terms. "I have . . . put My name there forever, and My eyes and My heart will be there perpetually."[29] John movingly writes of his vision of the City at the end of Revelation.

Come, I will show you the bride, the Lamb's wife.
And he carried me away in the Spirit to a great and high mountain,
and showed me the great city, the holy Jerusalem,
descending out of heaven from God.[30]

The city where God is pleased to dwell
    the place that has caught His eyes and heart
        the place where He has put His name
           is . . . us.

Jesus was taken up on a high mountain too; but He wasn't shown His Bride. Scripture says that Satan showed Him all of the kingdoms of the world, offering them to Jesus in place of waiting for the Bride—the new Jerusalem—that God wanted to give Him.

In essence, Jesus was shown what He could have had. How often I have seen men and women who never marry because they're afraid they will miss out on something better. So they keep looking, and miss out on the joy of committing to one.

Similarly, Jesus was tempted to keep looking. The Adversary was tempting Jesus to turn away from the city that is His future—the city that comes down from heaven—His Bride. "You can have all of this!" the evil one murmured. "Why settle for one when you can have many?"

Of course this came at the price of denying the Lord, and worshiping the Adversary.

Jesus' response was immediate: "Away with you, Satan! For it is written, 'You shall worship the LORD your God, and Him only you shall serve.'"[31] We were made for only one. One God. One Bride. Jesus knew that. He offered His worship to God alone, and He saved Himself for us. Like Abraham, He "waited for the city which has foundations, whose builder and maker *is* God."[32]

There is a river whose streams shall make glad the city of God,
The holy place of the tabernacle of the Most High.
God is in the midst of her, she shall not be moved.[33]

O Lord, hear! O Lord, forgive! O Lord, listen and act!
Do not delay for Your own sake, my God,
for Your city and Your people are called by Your name.[34]

For they call themselves after the holy city,
and lean on the God of Israel;
the LORD *of hosts is His name.*[35]

I will write on him . . . the name of the city of My God.

Three months before Scott went to be with the Lord, Jesus changed my name. I was at a conference when the Lord whispered into my heart, "Beginning today, I'm going to call you Rebecca." I had completely forgotten the incident that I described at the beginning of this chapter, and my only thought at the moment was, *Wow . . . the Lord finally answered the Becki/Rebecca debate.*

Months later, my life was in tremendous upheaval and transition. Scott had passed away, and everything was in flux. One day, I was cleaning out files, getting ready to move, and I came across a Post-it that was stuck inside of a desk drawer. It said,

I call you "Scott Bauer."

I don't know if it was the trauma of the season, but I honestly couldn't remember what that note was talking about. But—it was in my handwriting, and I had obviously saved it for a reason. So I stuck it on top of the desk to think about—and to see if I could remember why that sticky note was important. About a week later, I remembered and began to weep as I realized:

God had given me a new name for a new season.

I've known a lot of people who have changed their name for various reasons, so I'm not suggesting anything by this other than what the Lord said to me, and how He chose to work in my life. But the significance for me, and my journey, was unmistakable: He called me "Scott Bauer" when Scott and I were one. He also knew that Scott's home-going appointment was near at hand, and He gave me a new name. God saw what was ahead, and He was preparing me for it, though I couldn't have realized it at the time.

It was one of His first redemptive actions as I stepped into a new season of life:

I will write on him my new name.

1. 1 Samuel 16:7.
2. Genesis 2:23.
3. See Genesis 3:9.
4. Genesis 3:12.
5. 1 Corinthians 15:45.
6. See Ephesians 5:25.
7. 1 Peter 3:7.
8. See Revelation 5:12.
9. Revelation 3:7-13.
10. Matthew 1:21.
11. Philippians 2:9-11.
12. Acts 4:12.
13. See Acts 3:6; 4:30; 9:27; 16:18.
14. See Song of Songs 1:3.
15. Psalm 116:13.
16. Psalm 91:14.
17. Song of Songs 8:6.
18. Isaiah 43:1.
19. Genesis 10:25.
20. Genesis 17:5.
21. David Aune, *Word Biblical Commentary,* vol. 52A, Revelation 1–5 (Dallas, TX: Word Books, 1997), p. 244.
22. Genesis 32:27-28.
23. See Genesis 41:45.
24. See Mark 3:17; John 1:42.
25. 1 Chronicles 4:9.
26. 1 Chronicles 4:10.
27. Isaiah 62:2.
28. Isaiah 56:5.
29. 1 Kings 9:3.
30. Revelation 21:9-10.
31. Matthew 4:10.
32. Hebrews 11:10.
33. Psalm 46:4-5.
34. Daniel 9:19.
35. Isaiah 48:2.

Encountering Him

I DIDN'T CATCH YOUR NAME . . .

The first time I ever saw a meaning given to my name, I was 10 years old. The thing I read said that "Rebecca" meant "a noose." Gee . . . great. From that moment on, I decided I didn't like my name.

It was years before I ever looked up my name again or studied its meaning. What I found astounded me: I have never again been able to find that one dreadful meaning of my name. And believe me . . . I've looked.

As I studied, however, I began to see the prophetic significance of my name, and how my name linked to what God had called me to do and to teach. The Lord taught me things about my name, and has continued to do so; and I've come to love my name.

I also began to make "the study of your name" an assignment in one of the classes I teach. Along the way, I've discovered that a lot of people don't like their names. I've also come to believe that none of us is named by accident. Regardless of how our parents selected the names we were given, God knew our names before we were born.

Before I formed you in the womb I knew you.[1]

Before I was born the LORD called me;
From my birth he has made mention of my name.[2]

Here are a couple of guidelines as you begin your study:

1. Look up your name. You can find loads of websites that give the meanings of names. Look at several. Often, you will find several meanings for a name. Which one is the Lord pressing into your heart?

2. Then look up applicable Scripture. For example, my name, Rebecca, is actually in the Bible, so the stories of Rebekah have become very special to me. But don't limit it to that. Look up character traits that have to do with the meaning

of your name. Or simply see if that word is used in Scripture. For instance, "Stephen" means "crown," and that word is used in Scripture. How is it used? What might that mean for you and your life?

3. Finally, write about something the Lord taught you about your name. How has that character trait or word been used throughout your life?

4. One word of caution: Every time I give this assignment, I have students who come to me concerned because their name has a seemingly negative meaning. So just remember that we can learn by comparison and by contrast; what you *want* to be versus what you *don't want* to be. By way of example, one of the names that regularly comes up is "Mary," which means bitter. So what does God call us to be instead of bitter? And look at what He did at the waters of Marah when Israel was in the wilderness. He stepped in and made them sweet.[3] Names with negative meanings do not imply that you are negative. Rather it points to redemptive activity that God wants to flow in and through you.

After writing this assignment, one of my students wrote about the difference that understanding her name made for her:

This [assignment] made me realize that I'm not just some girl with a common name, but that my name is the title of my story and the plans God has for me. My name describes who I am and what I will do. It describes what God is going to do through me for other people. It makes me feel like I actually have meaning and a place in the story of this world. That I actually am a chapter in this big book of different stories that are different from mine but all with just as much importance and meaning.

When I finally started studying my own name, I discovered that it literally meant "bound," and among other figurative meanings it meant to "captivate (or bind or fetter) by beauty." Well . . . okay. I could accept that. Yet I wanted the Lord to teach me something more. Though, over time, the Lord has ministered Scriptures to me about my name, what immediately leapt to my mind was an old hymn. And I learned that being "bound" can be a good thing.

O to grace how great a debtor
daily I'm constrained to be!
Let Thy goodness, like a fetter,
bind my wandering heart to Thee.
Prone to wander, Lord, I feel it,
prone to leave the God I love;
here's my heart, O take and seal it,
seal it for Thy courts above.[4]

Knowing about our name helps us to accept who God has made us, and helps us to boldly step into ministry as citizens of His city. But knowing about His name is important too. Scripture also tells us that "those who know Your name will put their trust in You."[5] The next part of this chapter's encounter is to get to know the names of the Lord. Scripture uses dozens of names for God, but I'm only going to point out one.

In Exodus, God revealed Himself as "I Am." Inherent in that name is the fact that each day we face, He promises "I Am" whatever you need. Each of His names in Scripture presents us with another facet of His character.

What do you need today? Learn about His name. It helps us to know Him better and trust Him more.

Entire books have been written on the topic of the names of God, but you can easily find a list online. I've listed several of God's names given in the book of Revelation to get you started:

- Almighty—Revelation 1:8
- Alpha—Revelation 1:8
- Amen—Revelation 3:14
- Beginning—Revelation 21:6
- End—Revelation 21:6
- Faithful and True Witness—Revelation 3:14
- King of kings—Revelation 19:16
- Lion of the Tribe of Judah—Revelation 5:5

- Lord of lords—Revelation 19:16
- Morning Star—Revelation 22:16
- Omega—Revelation 1:8
- Root of David—Revelation 22:16
- Ruler of God's Creation—Revelation 3:14

1. Jeremiah 1:5.
2. Isaiah 49:1, *NIV*.
3. See Exodus 15:23-25.
4. "Come, Thou Fount," lyrics by Robert Robinson.
5. Psalm 9:10.

THE PARTNERSHIP

One day, Kyle came home talking about a beautiful girl he had met. Her name was Teresa. (Our son Kyle is bilingual, and at the time, he was attending our Spanish congregation so he could work on his language skills.) We, of course, started asking questions about this girl who had caught his eye. It turns out they met at church and were both singing on the worship team. And—Teresa was in the United States illegally.

Teresa's family had brought her here when she was a child. They entered the country legally; they just never left. We had heard stories of "marriages of convenience" to get a green card. We had even counseled people who had faced this situation. And we were more than a little concerned. We wanted our son to marry the woman he loved, but we wanted to be certain that this was love. Over time, we discovered this was, indeed, the case—they were crazy about each other!

In the process of their courtship, though, I learned a lot. I learned a lot of Spanish for one thing, but not very well (my son clearly didn't inherit his language skills from me). I can understand quite a bit, though, if you talk slowly enough. *¡Despacio, por favor!*

I also learned how difficult we make it for people to immigrate to our country. (Unbelievable, since unless you're descended from First Peoples, we have all descended from immigrants.) At one point, Teresa turned in paperwork to process residency and was actually notified by letter that she would hear from that department again— *in 10 years.*

Nope. We don't make it easy at all.

I also learned that my son has excellent discernment in character and excellent taste in choosing a wife.

As a couple, they checked out how to process Teresa's paperwork so that as soon as they were married they could begin to file for her residency. Then, 5 years later, she became a citizen. While she was originally told that she would be contacted in 10 years, marriage made the process go much faster.

Marriage brought about partnership—with a spouse and with a nation.

It reminds me of the process we go through when Jesus selects a bride:

> You were without Christ, being aliens from the commonwealth of Israel and strangers from the covenants of promise, having no hope and without God in the world. But now in Christ Jesus you who once were far off have been brought near by the blood of Christ . . . Now, therefore, you are no longer strangers and foreigners, but fellow citizens with the saints and members of the household of God.[1]

We, too, were foreigners—unable to get the help we needed, unable to fend for ourselves. We were unable to acquire "legal status" until Jesus poured out His life for us and accepted us as His Beloved. He loved us before we loved Him, and He chose us—illegal aliens—as His Bride. Now we have been brought near . . .

> into His heart,
> into His family,
> into His Kingdom.

....

As surely as being accepted in the Beloved[2] provides us with a family and Kingdom, it also provides us with a purpose and call. Jesus invites us not only into relationship, but into partnership.

The Bible says that Jesus laid hold of us for a purpose[3]—and that it is for more than just having a passionate relationship. Relationships are intended to result in partnership, to go somewhere, to produce growth. It's expected—the obvious result of relationship is fruitfulness. Look at how Jesus describes this connection of relationship, partnership and fruitfulness:

> *Abide in Me, and I in you.*
> *As the branch cannot bear fruit of itself, unless it abides in the vine,*
> *neither can you, unless you abide in Me.*
> *"I am the vine, you are the branches.*
> *He who abides in Me, and I in him, bears much fruit;*
> *for without Me you can do nothing."*[4]

We learned this in our own lives. Several years into our marriage, Scott and I were both coming up on graduations (Scott from seminary, me from Bible college), and we were moving to the next stage of our life. It was time to start a family. As we talked about timing and finances—the practicalities of considering this next big step—we realized that we also felt something more. We discovered that our love for each other had grown to a point that we simply needed more people to share it with! So we began adding children to our family. *Because love grew, it had to be shared.* The outflow of the love of relationship is intended to make a difference in the world around us—it's intended to be shared.

Jesus laid hold of us for a purpose.

In order for us to fulfill the purpose and partnership, and share His love with the world, Jesus has put the riches of His Kingdom at our disposal. Scripture tells us that we have been given the riches of His glory,[5] His wisdom[6] and His grace.[7] As if that isn't enough, here's the carte blanche statement: We've also been given the "unsearchable riches of Christ."[8]

This doesn't even begin to address the fact that all of the legal paperwork has been filed for us. We have been brought into association with the Bridegroom and into every resource of His Kingdom.[9] There was a law of sin and death that we were going to have to answer to, until Jesus answered it for us.[10]

To top it off, He invites us to rule with Him. He is King of kings, and He has chosen us to be His Bride. I've watched enough royal weddings to know that when a king chooses a bride, she becomes a queen. He has raised us up to sit with Him in heavenly places,[11] and called us to join Him in

Partnership. Life. Purpose. Riches. Fruitfulness. Rulership.

....

Scott's family moved cross-country—from Virginia to California—the summer between his junior and senior years of high school. That is a terrible time to move a young person—especially someone like Scott who had his whole life already mapped out. University. Economics. Congress. This was his long-range plan. Then his family moved.

That move changed everything about his life.

When I met him, about two years after they arrived in California, I thought Scott was a really great guy. The more I got to know him, the more my opinion was confirmed. But I had predetermined that if Scott ever asked me out, I wasn't going to go. Our lives were headed in different directions. I was aimed at Bible college and ministry, and though Scott now lived in a different state, his goal was still University. Economics. Congress.

That wasn't the direction I was headed, so I figured why start something that wasn't going to go anywhere. Except that the Lord told me to go out with Scott.

I believe God's exact words were: *Date who I tell you to date; it's My job to fulfill My word in your life.*

I learned an important lesson that day: I cannot manipulate God's promises or make them come to pass by my own efforts or planning. My job is obedience. Pure and simple. His job is to get me to where I'm supposed to be.

So with that understanding, when Scott asked me for a date, I said yes.

Knowing that it's God's job to fulfill His word in my life, I shouldn't have been surprised when just a few weeks later the Lord called Scott into ministry and completely changed the direction of his life.

Though Scott and I still had a few months to go before we decided that we were serious about each other, God was already at work dovetailing ministry call and setting a solid relationship into place. We both felt called to ministry, so that our involvement in it was always as partners, as a team, a joint effort. Along with finding a bride, God brought about a partnership and purpose that Scott had never dreamed of.

Relationship. Partnership. Rulership. Purpose.

This is what Jesus was offering to the church at Thyatira.

And it's what He offers us. It's all at our disposal. But He calls us—He *longs* for us—to step into partnership with Him, and to accept the same promise He gave to the Thyatirans: *I will give power over the nations . . .*

> *Ask of Me, and I will give You the nations for Your inheritance,*
> *And the ends of the earth for Your possession.*[12]

It is your Father's good pleasure to give you the kingdom.[13]

You shall be witnesses to Me in Jerusalem, and in all Judea and Samaria, and to the end of the earth.[14]

....

We're called to partner with our Bridegroom; yet the church at Thyatira faced two realities directly opposed to allowing that partnership to take place. The first was opposition from within—a false doctrine that was drawing away some of the believers into an indulgent and unrestrained lifestyle endorsed by a self-proclaimed prophetess. "Partnering" with this doctrine involved sexual immorality.

The other opposition came from the culture, and it came in the form of trade guilds or unions. The challenge was that each guild had a patron god. If you didn't belong to one of the guilds, your business would suffer; but if you did belong, "members counted themselves to be in the service of the god through their daily work."[15] It was partnership through idolatry.

Through it all, Jesus called to this church, "if you keep My works . . . I will give power over the nations." A promise of rulership. A promise of partnership.

> And to the angel of the church in Thyatira write, "These things says the Son of God, who has eyes like a flame of fire, and His feet like fine brass: 'I know your works, love, service, faith, and your patience; and as for your works, the last are more than the first. Nevertheless I have a few things against you, because you allow that woman Jezebel, who calls herself a prophetess, to teach and seduce My servants to commit sexual immorality and eat things sacrificed to idols. And I gave her time to repent of her sexual immorality, and she did not repent. Indeed I will cast her into a sickbed, and those who commit adultery with her into great tribulation, unless they repent of their deeds. I will kill her children with death, and all the churches shall know that I am He who searches the minds and hearts. And I will give to each one of you according to your works. Now to you I say, and to the rest in Thyatira, as many as do not have this doctrine, who have not

known the depths of Satan, as they say, I will put on you no
other burden. But hold fast what you have till I come. And he
who overcomes, and keeps My works until the end, to him I will
give power over the nations—"He shall rule them with a rod of
iron; they shall be dashed to pieces like the potter's vessels"—as
I also have received from My Father; and I will give him the
morning star. "He who has an ear, let him hear what the Spirit
says to the churches." ' "[16]

Rights and Privileges

We've been brought into His Kingdom. Partnership is offered. Jesus
promises power over the nations. We're seated with Him in heavenly
places.

Partnership. Purpose. Calling. Rulership.

Like the Thyatirans. Like Teresa. Like Esther.

Esther is a perfect example of partnership, though I'm sure that neither she nor the king of Persia ever expected it. It just wasn't being done.

She had been made queen and really could have settled down to a
pretty nice existence with anything she wanted at her command. Well,
okay—she was at the whim of the king, but he had a whole harem he
could call. In fact, at the point that God brought her into partnership,
the king had not called for her in 30 days. All to say, she had a lot of
luxury at her fingertips, and a lot of time on her hands.

But God had bigger plans for Esther, and He has bigger plans for
you too.

Most of us know Esther's story well. The king needed a new queen
and had called for a nationwide search for the most beautiful girls in the
land. Considering the age when most girls were married in that day, Esther would probably have been between 12 and 15 years old when she
was brought to the court.

A few years later, when she was challenged to save her people, she
was most likely only around 20—a shocking age to have the lives of mil-
lions of people resting on her shoulders.

And she had a choice.

Actually, she had several choices: She could have backed away from
the responsibility. She could have retreated into luxury. She could have

wrung her hands and defaulted to indecision or fear. She could even have wallowed in unworthiness: "I'm just a kid. What do I know about affairs of state?"

All of those were options, but they all ended the same way: with inaction on the part of the bride, the queen. We're faced with similar choices. Will we "default"? Or will we take the risk and step into destiny, partnership, strength and rulership?

The turning point for Esther came with her cousin's words:

> *If you remain completely silent at this time,*
> *relief and deliverance will arise . . . from another place. . . .*
> *Yet who knows whether*
> *you have come to the kingdom for such a time as this?*[17]

Deliverance could have risen from another place. But Esther took the risk and went before the king, and salvation flowed because of her actions. It's a moving story of the miraculous hand of God working on behalf of His people.

Through a young girl.

That isn't the end of the story. We know the outcome so well that we tend to overlook the fact that the king suddenly realized that he had more than just a cute girl in Esther. He also had a tremendous ally. And that brings about a partnership on another scale.

Eventually, she was given the king's signet ring to freely do business in his name. That ring gave her authority to sign legal documents in the name of the ruler of the then-known world:

> *You yourselves write a decree concerning the Jews, as you please,*
> *in the king's name, and seal it with the king's signet ring;*
> *for whatever is written in the king's name*
> *and sealed with the king's ring no one can revoke . . .*
> *Then Queen Esther . . . wrote with full authority.*[18]

> *Partnership. Rulership. Full authority.*

Steel Magnolias

It took the king of Persia a long time to learn something about women that my son Brian learned when he was still in high school.

Scott and I, like most parents, kept an eagle eye on which girls seemed to seek out either of our sons. One day, at a school event, a very pretty girl came up to Brian and chatted for a few minutes. After she had gone, I wanted to get Brian's thoughts on her, so I commented as casually as I could, "She's cute." He responded, "Yeah . . . but she's dumb."

(You would have to know Brian to know that he wasn't making some kind of a "girls have cooties" statement; he literally didn't think she was smart. Thankfully, I have no recollection of who that girl was. I don't know whether she was bright or not but, regardless, it's still the impression she made on Brian that day.)

Later, I told Scott about the incident. He smiled and said, "Good! Once you find out that 'smart' is important, you're never attracted by 'only pretty' again."

The issue isn't that God will tell you to marry someone you aren't attracted to; His plan is to give you the whole package. That proved to be true in Brian's case—Melissa is beautiful *and* brilliant! The bigger issue is that

Jesus wants to empower His Bride to become His partner.

That kind of partnership requires the participation of both members of a couple—in this case, you (or me) and Jesus. He has already taken action. Now it's your turn.

What are you going to do?

Rulership isn't generally handed to someone who is content to sit around and just be "the beautiful Bride." Jesus is looking for strength in a partner. He's looking for someone who will reach out, take hold of the resources at hand and become a partner. He's looking for someone who will rule and reign with Him.

Often, however, we don't look for strength in a partner. In fact, we often don't even want it—in ourselves or in someone else—let alone in a partner. "Being strong" pushes us out of our comfort zones, and requires something of us.

An older gentleman in our church once told me that he wanted a wife who would "keep things clean, was young enough to still bear children and who wouldn't challenge him." Well—at least he was honest. But truth be told, it sounded to me like he was looking for a concubine. He wanted someone who would serve him, not partner with him. Women do the same thing. They look for someone who is a "romantic lead" but won't confront them to grow. In both of these scenarios, the issue becomes our own comfort, not our service to another. Taking rather than giving.

Our Bridegroom, Jesus, approaches things from an opposite point of view. He said that He came not to be served, but to serve.[19] True strength and true partnership will always look for ways to serve. He is looking for the same thing in His Bride.

"Steel magnolias" seems a fitting description of what the Lord calls His Bride to be. The term is an idiom meaning a blend of strength and beauty. We've already talked about not being "just pretty," but remember that whatever the Lord puts His hand on will become beautiful. That means us too.

But He's also made His Bride strong. The Bible describes her as warrior, athlete and priest.[20] He isn't looking for a passive, mindless, wishy-washy shrinking violet.

The Bible talks about "men of valor," and I think that phrase describes Jesus perfectly! That word—"valor"—literally means "a force." It is, in fact, the same word used to describe the Proverbs 31 woman— *Who can find a woman of valor?* Who can find a woman who is a *force?* Where can the man of valor—Jesus—find a woman who is His match?

A woman of valor. A force. Strength and beauty. Steel magnolias.
He's looking for us.

Tempered Steel

Strength in women sometimes makes people nervous. And, gentlemen, don't lose me here! When I talk about strength in women, I'm talking about us—all of us, male and female—the Bride of Christ. Every one of us has to make the decision for "strength," because our human nature will always regress to its own comfort, if possible— whether that's through passivity or iron-fisted control. When we look at Jesus, we see that strength always serves.

If you want to be great in the Kingdom,
learn to be the servant of all.[21]

In Thyatira, they had a reason to be concerned about "strength in women." A woman in their church was teaching things contrary to Scripture. She was "a force." She had been able to gain a following, but the Lord refers to her as "Jezebel"—a reference to an Old Testament queen who led Israel into idolatry, rebellion and murder. The presence of this woman in the church makes an important point: Though God made His daughters to be strong women of valor, their strength can also be misused and abused.

This woman stands in direct contrast to what we saw in Esther. Esther boldly stepped into partnership; Jezebel grasped after a following. Esther went before a pagan king, pleading for the life of a nation; Jezebel was seeking to mislead the people of God. Esther was willing to give up her life if need be; Jezebel was given an opportunity to repent, but she turned it down.

God made His Bride strong, and it's not something He's afraid of. But strength must always be used wisely, and within the boundaries of His Word. Both Ephesians 5:22 and Colossians 3:18 state that wives are to be in submission to their own husbands. This does not say that all women are in submission to all men. That would be a rather scary proposition. No. We are to submit to our own husband "as to the Lord."

Over the years, I have seen this concept misapplied to an extreme, and it is an abuse of God's intent for submission. I've seen women treated as though they can't do anything, decide anything, accomplish anything without asking permission. I once heard of a woman who wouldn't give her children a snack until she had called her husband at work and asked if that was all right; another woman wasn't allowed to call to have the heat repaired because "only the husband could do that." That is an abuse of submission, as much as "Jezebel" was an abuse of strength. Living as a submitted woman does not mean that your theme song is now "if I only had a brain." As with many other concepts in Scripture, submission is intended to release, not restrict. *It is intended to redeem, to draw us back to the original intention of marriage.* It is intended to help draw couples into partnership, not servitude.

I believe that God set things up the way He did to address what the man and the woman didn't do at their temptation and fall. When the woman ate the forbidden fruit, she stepped away from God-ordained partnership—she acted on her own. The man didn't lead either. Could Adam have "paid the price" for his bride? It's what Jesus did, as "the last Adam."[22] Instead, he decided he would just do what the woman said. He would eat the fruit too. The woman acted on her own; the man didn't lead. The woman was deceived; the man knowingly disobeyed.

So God set this order in place: Woman—you didn't work with your partner, and I'm now challenging that independence. I am setting in place a compulsory cooperation. Man—you didn't lead, and I'm going to challenge that passivity, so now I am setting in place a compulsory leadership. They were created for partnership, and the Lord set in order a plan to redeem them back to that.

The word "submission," used in New Testament times, was actually a military term and means "to arrange under." Ephesians not only describes how husbands and wives are to relate to one another, but it boldly states that we are to "submit one to another." It's a skill we all have to learn as the Bride of Christ. And there's a "senior partner." We all do well to defer to Him!

Heirs Together

In the previous chapter we talked a little bit about the first couple: they were called Adam. They shared everything—even a name. But the first couple can also teach us about partnership:

> God created man in His own image . . .
> male and female He created them.
> Then God blessed them, and God said to them,
> "Be fruitful and multiply;
> fill the earth and subdue it;
> have dominion."[23]

> Power over the nations.

One chapter later, we have a close-up view of the creation of the man and the woman. God formed the man and breathed life into him; then He formed the woman from the rib of the man. The "rib" and an unfortunate English translation of the Hebrew have sometimes diminished people's view of the role of the woman. We picture a "little helper." Yet the Hebrew words that are translated "helpmeet"—*ezer kenegdo*—are very strong words, literally meaning "a help who is comparable to." There was nothing diminished about the creation of the woman. She was comparable to the man. She was his counterpart.

Love Letter

I saw cards too mushy and cards too silly. I saw cards too pretty and cards too old. I saw cards too perfect and cards too ugly. But I never found one that said or looked exactly the way I feel about you.

You are the joy of my life and my best friend. You are my passion and my encourager. You are the best thing God could ever do for me, and you are my love. You are my personal instructor and my partner. You are the one to share my pain and you make my joy indescribable. You are my help and you are my future.

sgb to rlb
July 1992, 16th wedding anniversary

As Jesus' Bride, He calls us to the same activities to which the first couple were called: partnership, dominion, fruitfulness. If you're married, you are learning about this partnership with Jesus by doing marriage in a day-to-day, 24/7 relationship! The Lord has you on a journey to move you back toward that original intent with your spouse—*heirs together*.

If you are single, you are learning about this partnership on an adventurous one-on-one journey with Jesus. You are learning a dependence on Him and an ability to hear His voice at an ever-deepening level, because it is just the two of you.

I have learned about partnering with Jesus on both of those journeys—married and single. They are very different, but they are both wonderful.

We are children of God, and if children, then heirs—
Heirs of God and joint heirs with Christ.[24]

We are heirs together with Jesus.

Swept off Your Feet

During Jesus' ministry, a woman came to His feet, not sure she would be accepted, let alone partnered with. She broke open and poured out everything she had—a bottle of expensive perfume. Scripture states that the host at the dinner had not provided for the washing of Jesus' feet. In our automobile-and-rapid-transit era, we don't always appreciate how grimy and gritty that would have felt. At a time in history when you walked everywhere and wore sandals, having your guests' feet washed was common courtesy. A courtesy not extended to Jesus.

Nor can we fully appreciate what this woman gave up. The perfume was probably worth about a year's salary—obviously a rare commodity at the time.[25]

But she came.

She came to Jesus' feet. To get to His feet, she would have had to get off of hers. This wasn't the moment to "stand strong"; this was the moment to—in humility, worship and love—go to the only place that provided

Hope. Acceptance. Forgiveness.

On the floor at someone's feet is not the place where we think of strong people going. In fact, when we hear this story, we rarely think of this woman as a strong woman. But true strength knows how to seek help, when to serve, when to give up, when to submit. And true strength also knows where to go.

His feet. Broken. Poured out.

The night before Jesus was crucified, He washed His disciples' feet. The Church had not been birthed. There was no Bride yet—only these 12 men to whom Jesus' message would be entrusted. They were all of the Bride that existed on that day. And Jesus kneels to serve them. True strength knows when to serve, when to give up and where to go.

He was on His way to the cross, to pay the Bride price for . . . *us*.

And now He is looking for partners like the woman that night so long ago who broke open her costliest treasure and poured it out for Him. Will you answer His call?

To give. To serve. To be broken. To be poured out. To accept partnership.

....

Partnership doesn't happen overnight. It grows, along with love. It's richness and depth develops over time. We began our study of the letters by looking at *"first love, first works."* But now Jesus says to the church at Thyatira, *"as for your works, the last are more than the first."*

Last works.

Like fine wine, the last is better than the first.

Jesus offers here an acknowledgement that works flowing from passion over a long period of time will issue forth in the promise the Thyatirans received: *"he who overcomes, and keeps My works until the end, to him I will give power over the nations."*

Love grows. Love works. Love partners.

Scott and I had quite a life—serving, loving, giving, growing, partnering—in our home and in our church. We raised a family, pastored a church, walked through joy, experienced some trials. We buried a brother, faced surgery and survived an earthquake. We moved, bought a home, taught kids how to drive, planted lawns, owned dogs, traveled, laughed, played, worked. Laundry. School plays. Baseball. Dance lessons.

Graduations. Christmases. Engagements. Birthdays. Weddings.

We would occasionally have people ask us how we got it all done— how we accomplished everything and maintained a happy, healthy family too.

Our answer always came back to Jesus. We started each day at Jesus' feet, because if you begin there, He will always give you something to pour out to the world. Partnering with Him begins in laying down our strength and taking up His so that we, like Him, can be poured out to the nations.

*My grace is sufficient for you, for My strength
is made perfect in weakness.*[26]

*But those who wait on the LORD shall renew their strength;
They shall mount up with wings like eagles.*[27]

1. Ephesians 2:12-13,19.
2. See Ephesians 1:6.
3. See Philippians 3:12.
4. John 15:4-5.
5. See Romans 9:23.
6. See Romans 11:33.
7. See Ephesians 1:7.
8. See Ephesians 3:8.
9. See also Romans 5:8-10; 2 Corinthians 5:19; Colossians 1:19-20.
10. See Romans 8:2.
11. Ephesians 2:6; see also Ephesians 1:20-21.
12. Psalm 2:8.
13. Luke 12:32.
14. Acts 1:8.
15. Stanley MacNair, *To the Churches, with Love* (Los Angeles: Judson Press, 1960), p. 78.
16. Revelation 2:18-29.
17. Esther 4:14.
18. Esther 8:8; 9:29.
19. See Matthew 20:28.
20. See 2 Timothy 2:3; Hebrews 12:1; Revelation 5:10.
21. See Mark 10:44.
22. See Romans 5:12-21; 1 Corinthians 15.
23. Genesis 1:27-28.
24. Romans 8:16-17.
25. See Luke 7:36-50.
26. 2 Corinthians 12:9.
27. Isaiah 40:31.

Encountering Him

BROKEN FOR THE WORLD

When Jesus was here on earth, He multiplied bread for thousands. He took something very simple, very basic, very limited—and under His touch, broke it and brought provision to many.[1]

Very simple. Very basic. Very limited.

Sounds like me! It probably sounds like you too.

We are so afraid that Jesus won't be able to use us; yet, like the bread, He puts His touch on us, breaks us and makes us so much more than we could be by ourselves. And He uses us to minister to multitudes.

Multitudes?

Yes. Multitudes.

Your "multitude" may seem very small to you today. It may be the people you work with, or your preschool-aged children, or your class at school or the people you pass in your neighborhood. It may be your child's teacher or the checker at the grocery store or your boss.

God multiplies Himself through you to them.

Jesus was broken for the world in sacrifice. It's how He won His Bride. But now, as His Bride, He asks us if we will be broken for the world too.

In this chapter's Encounter, I'm going to ask you to simply spend time with Jesus breaking bread—as surely as He broke bread on that hillside two millennia ago. It's a time to ask Him some questions and let Him supply you with answers. We so often doubt our ability to reach the world around us. But we are Jesus' Bride, and we represent Him to everyone we meet.

As you break bread with Him, you may want to pray out loud. Or you may decide you would like to pray silently. Sometimes in those moments, I call it "thinking in the presence of Jesus." He's there. I'm there. Resting in His presence.

So get some bread, and "break bread" with Jesus. When I have done this, I personally like to use pita bread, though any bread will do—from Wonder bread, to homemade bread (yum!), to rustic-style artisan breads.

And then listen for His voice.

On the day of Jesus' resurrection, the Bible says that on the road to Emmaus, He was made known to the two disciples "in the breaking of bread."[2] In the breaking of bread is a moment to ask the Lord to make things clear. While there are always things we want to know from Jesus, today I'm asking you to focus on how He wants you to partner with Him in reaching your world, your family—the realm of your influence, the people within your reach.

Ask Him:

- How do You want to multiply me to the world?
- What are You giving me to give away?
- Are there areas of serving that You have called me to, but I haven't heard or answered?

Let Him be known to you in the breaking of bread, and let Him put His touch on your life to multiply you to the world.

---

1. See Matthew 14:15-21.
2. Luke 24:35.

Epilogue

SWEET SOMETHINGS

One day when my sons were about 10 and 11 years old, they decided
to mount a revolt against chores. I've never been hesitant to assign
chores to my children; in fact, a friend and I decided we were going to
name our homes "Baby Boot Camp."

On *this* day—which we'll call "Revolt Saturday," I had lists ready.
Normally, I am an early riser. In fact, I rarely even use an alarm clock.
So by the time my kids were up, I had been up for hours, had already
done a lot of work, prepared their chore lists, prepared *my* chore list
(much longer than theirs), and when they finally crawled out of bed,
I was sitting down for a coffee break.

"It's not fair," my son announced. (Kids really like that word.)

"What's not fair?"

"You get to sit around and we have to do all of the work."

(*Really?* I asked myself.) Out loud I said, "Okay . . . I'll tell you
what. You have your list, and mine is in the kitchen. Go look at mine,
and if you would like to trade, I'll do it."

Off he went for inspection. And decided that his list wasn't so
bad after all!

Later that day, however, Scott heard about that interchange and
was less than pleased. He pulled both of the boys aside and started
questioning:

Who cooks dinner? Who makes breakfast? Who does laundry?
Who made your bedspreads? Who refinished your dresser? Who
dusts? Who vacuums? Who makes birthday cakes? Who cleans the
bathrooms? Who . . . ? You get the idea. He asked about 50 questions,
and the answer to every one of them was "Mom." By the time he was
done, even I was pretty impressed with myself!

And I felt very affirmed.

Scott always viewed what I did as equivalent with what he did.
We held the same life-goals, and we served them all the time. Whether
we were together or apart, whether we were at home, at church or at

the office, we both knew that we were investing in jointly held values. All of the time. Everywhere we were.

But beyond feeling affirmed, it encouraged me to know that

Scott knew my works.

....

I Know Your Works

Jesus knows our works, too, and He affirms that in each of the letters of Revelation:

I know your works.

"I know your works" is one of three phrases that appear in all seven of the letters to the churches. The Lord also makes promises to "the one who overcomes," and then encourages His people to "hear what the Spirit says to the churches." In this chapter, we will look at all three of these phrases, starting with Jesus' view of our works.

When Jesus says that He knows their works, He's saying much more than simply listing what they've been up to. And, because these letters have been viewed so negatively, even the listing of each church's works has been held up for criticism. For example, we focus on the fact that Sardis is dead, Philadelphia has only a little strength, and Laodicea is neither hot nor cold. Those things *were* true . . . but just criticizing them wasn't the point of why Jesus said what He did.

Jesus is writing to His Bride, and He wants to see her thrive. This acknowledgement of their works indicates that He knows what they are facing, He knows where they are, He knows how they got there and now, He's here to help. And notice please that He never tells them to stop working. Life involves work. But Jesus is acknowledging that each church faces its own challenge, and He sees all of it.

I know your works.

The church at Ephesus is commended. Jesus describes their patience and their stand against compromise and evil. Smyrna is clearly facing tribulation: Jesus describes their works as assault, poverty, prison and testing. Pergamos is facing tribulation, as well, but Jesus encourages them that He knows where they dwell—in a place of unmitigated evil. He knows what they face.

Thyatira's works are most highly commended—*your last works are more than the first*; while Sardis's works are the most dismal—incomplete, in fact, dying. Jesus is never there just to pronounce a death sentence—He's there to say there's still hope. In Him, there's always hope for resurrection!

Philadelphia is encouraged that though they "have a little strength," they have persevered and stood strong. Laodicea is told that they are neither hot nor cold. They haven't taken a strong stand—about anything.

All of these descriptions of how the churches are doing remind me of different things all of us face, and they contain the promise of the Lord to meet and strengthen us.

The church at Philadelphia had open doors in front of them. That's exciting! But they also had only "a little strength." There was opportunity, but they were simply too weak and weary to go on. There are times when I've been weary in the battle too. In those times, as He spoke to this church, Jesus says,

I know where you're weary. I know you're weak.
My strength is made perfect in your weakness. Lean on Me.

Sometimes we simply need to be affirmed. We've worked hard, and it feels like no one notices or knows. The churches in Ephesus and Thyatira could have easily felt this way. Jesus encourages,

I know what you're doing and you're doing it right.
I see your faithfulness.

Smyrna and Pergamos were facing tremendous assault. There are times in life when it seems that everything is going wrong and everyone is against you. Jesus knows what this is like; He's been there too.

I know what you face, I know where you are, and I'm here with you.

The Sardians dealt with the scariest scenario—everything looks fine, but lurking below the surface is something that will bring death. The things they are doing are incomplete, because they are not seeing the whole picture. *If we just keep moving, everything will be fine.* You can see Jesus standing in front of them with tears in His eyes, begging them to stand still and take stock.

I'm not done with you yet . . . but you need to reevaluate.

Finally, the Laodiceans are just breezing through life, not making a firm stand on anything. *Everything's just fine, thanks!* Jesus challenges their denial and indecision: You "do not know that you are wretched, miserable, poor, blind, and naked." You think you're fine—but you're not.

I know where you're in danger. I know where the compromise is.
Turn your hearts to Me and let Me in.

Have you ever faced what any of these churches faced? I know I have. And, like them, I've faced them while I've been trying to serve the Lord. I don't know about you, but sometimes it's a comfort to know that Jesus really knows what we are facing. When we're dealing with

Weakness. Assault. Weariness. Death. Loneliness.
Faithfulness. Patience. Open doors.

It's good to know that He knows our works.

Several years ago, Pastor Robert Morris spoke at our church. During his sermon, he shared about a time in his life when the Lord had challenged him and his wife, Debbie, to "give everything." As soon as he shared the example, I could feel myself clinging to my little savings account. (As though that was ever going to protect me from anything.) Of course, I know that isn't how we are supposed to live. God is my provider, but He will insist on correct priority. He isn't intimidated by money, but neither does He want it to be first in our lives.

At the end of the sermon, as Pastor Robert usually does, he said, "I want you to bow your head and ask the Holy Spirit what He's saying to you today." I bowed my head, certain that I knew that God was going to tell me to "give everything." But I asked anyway, and what the Lord said stunned me.

You did give everything.
And you didn't complain, or get angry or bitter.

I sat there completely overwhelmed. It wasn't the answer I had expected, but what astounded me was the fact that *He knew*. He knew what the loss of Scott had cost me, and He valued it.

He knew my works.
And He knows yours too.

Love Letter

Scott was my greatest cheerleader for whatever new venture I wanted to try. Like the Lord, he always encouraged me to become more than I was. He challenged me to confront fear, learn new things, grow in self-confidence and pursue continued freedom in the Lord. Even when he was afraid I might face failure or disappointment, he spoke words of encouragement and support because he believed in me. Words cannot express how constantly amazing it was to me to have someone in my life who simply believed that "me and Jesus" could do anything.

There are things I've done that I would never have even tried if Scott hadn't been there cheering me on. Without that legacy, I would not be able to face today. And I am so deeply thankful for his faithfulness to me.

rlb, october 2003
sgb memorial bulletin

To Him Who Overcomes

Scott loved the fact that his ring had "nicks" in it. For years, I tried to get him to let me take it to a jeweler and have it polished up. No way. He would have none of it.

And he liked telling people about it—especially when he performed weddings. He would talk about the fact that his ring had on it "the marks of life." Those nicks all represented life, activity and work. It represented doing dishes, changing diapers, mowing lawns, playing baseball, helping kids with algebra, teaching kids to ride bikes, household repairs, paying bills, swimming.

(Can I also add that some of those nicks came from trips to the emergency room, cleaning up puke and swabbing toilets. Sometimes life just isn't pretty.)

All of those nicks stood for something; they all came at a price, and no matter what life threw at us—we overcame.

When Jesus talks about overcoming, He makes a lot of promises to *the one who overcomes*. He promises

> *Life—and life more abundant*
> *A crown and a throne—new rulership*
> *Manna—new provision*
> *The morning star—dawn of a new day*
> *White garments—new identity*
> *Announced before Father—security of relationship*
> *A pillar in God's presence—solid ground*

But like the nicks on Scott's ring, receiving those promises and rewards
> stands for something,
>> comes at a cost and
>>> requires the commitment to overcome.

Jesus said, "These things I have spoken to you, that in Me you may have peace. In the world you will have tribulation; but be of good cheer, I have overcome the world."[1] Jesus is the original Overcomer, and He's here to help us do the same.

So what is the tribulation that you've faced and overcome? Loss comes to all of us, and it comes in different packages. As I've already shared, my tribulation came through death.

Death isn't something we like to talk about. Yet Jesus calls us to die to ourselves, take up our cross daily and lay down our lives. It is only through dying to ourselves that we are ever able to enter into all that God has for us. Unless I die to *me*, I cannot become one with Him.

Becoming one with someone requires a death of sorts. And it is through dying that we truly live. "Jesus said to His disciples, 'If anyone desires to come after Me, let him deny himself, and take up his cross, and follow Me. For whoever desires to save his life will lose it, but whoever loses his life for My sake will find it.'"[2]

Following the death of my husband, I realized that while I didn't face death for myself, I did look death in the face and choose to not allow it to determine my future. That's only possible because God always brings life out of death. He *is* the resurrection and the life.

> *O Death where is your sting?*
> *O grave, where is your victory?*[3]

Death still happens—but the sting is gone. The grave still accepts a body—but the person isn't there; he's with the Lord. "Why do you look for the living among the dead?"[4]

> *God always brings life out of death.*

Love Letter

Friday morning, I went to the hospital early to sit and hold Scott's hand. I knew it was the last time I would be able to do so. As I sat there, I said to the Lord, "All I know to do is to keep clinging to Jesus." He immediately replied, "All other ground is sinking sand—even Scott." I knew what He meant. My life is to always be built on Jesus alone. No one else can provide a solid foundation for life.

rhb, october 2003
sgb memorial bulletin

There's more than one way to die besides physical death. There is the death of dreams, the death of relationships, the death of hope.

And Jesus calls us to overcome in those as well.

How easy it is for us to be hurt or disillusioned, and rather than reaching out to seek understanding and relationship, we separate ourselves from those who have wounded us. We are tempted to give place to independence, bitterness, fear and unforgiveness. We allow our world to grow ever smaller, ever more "self-sufficient," ever more insulated, safe behind our walls.

But the Lord calls us to live differently. He calls us to die to ourselves and overcome

- The need to be "right" (pride)
- The cutting, sarcastic remark that would be so satisfying to say (anger)
- The certainty that "I really understand everything about this situation" (judgmentalism)
- The desire to give that person "the cold shoulder" (unforgiveness)
- The human tendency to let our wound define us (clinging to the past)
- The desire to get even (vindictiveness)

Listen to what Jesus says:

> Unless a grain of wheat falls into the earth and dies,
> it remains alone; but if it dies,
> it bears much fruit.[5]

In forgiveness or fruitfulness, we are helpless without Him—helpless to heal our own hurts or a strained relationship. Whatever of your rights has been violated, whatever of your past hurt seems to linger, the Lord asks you to die to your right to be wounded, unforgiving, afraid. Whatever challenge you're facing with a co-worker, a friend or family member, He calls you to die to your right to be judgmental, vindictive or angry.

God takes "dying to self" even further. It isn't only grief, sorrow or separation. Death is also promise fulfilled. You see, as a bride I made a promise—till death do us part; but as a widow I fulfilled it. I "finished the race"; I was faithful to the end; I overcame.

Just like Jesus, who won us by giving His life.

The fact is that on the day of our wedding, when we declare our love for one another, few of us think about the day that we will see the triumph of the faithfulness of love. Though "till death do us part" is in the wedding vows, we glibly repeat the words to one another, not giving a thought to that "other day" when one of us will lay the other in the arms of Jesus. On our wedding day, we celebrate love. On that other day, we celebrate love of a different kind.

Love that endured.

Love that remained faithful.

Love that overcame.

'Til death do us part.

A hard day, yes. But look at what John wrote in the promise to the Bride as she comes to her Bridegroom:

Then I, John, saw the holy city, New Jerusalem, coming down out of heaven from God, prepared as a bride adorned for her husband. And I heard a loud voice from heaven saying, "Behold, the tabernacle of God is with men, and He will dwell with them, and they shall be His people. God Himself will be with them and be their God. And God will wipe away every tear from their eyes; there shall be no more death, nor sorrow, nor crying. There shall be no more pain, for the former things have passed away." Then He who sat on the throne said, "Behold, I make all things new." And He said to me, "Write, for these words are true and faithful."[6]

Faithful and true. No more tears. Overcomers.

Love Letter

You are the love of my life and the passion of my thought and heart. Eighteen years is not enough. But then neither will a lifetime suffice.

sgb to rlb

July 24, 1994, 18th wedding anniversary

Hear What the Spirit Says

I've never thought of myself as a nervous mother, but there was one thing I worried about with some regularity—my children's hearing.

I was always sure that there was something wrong. This came up enough times that Scott finally devised our own hearing test, so that I would quit worrying and stop hauling the kids off to the doctor.

One day, I couldn't get the kids to respond when I called them. (*Of course I couldn't; they were all glued to the TV set!*) I, once again, went to Scott with a concern that the kids' hearing was at risk. He tiptoed into the family room, where the TV was still blasting away. He stood about 20 feet behind them, and then at a zero decibel whisper, he said,

"Let's go to Disneyland."

Three heads instantly spun around.

Scott looked at me, rolled his eyes and said, "They're fine."

He also followed up with the kids about their responsiveness, and the fact that you always have to be listening. Even when you're doing something else. Our kids were obedient kids, but they, like us, can get "used to" a voice.

At the end of each letter, Jesus says:

"He who has an ear, let him hear what the Spirit says to the churches."

He isn't wondering if you have ears. He's asking if you're listening. A life-changing song for my dad was Audrey Mieir's "Listen for the Whispers." Jesus wants us to be so close and so attentive that He doesn't have to shout. He wants us to be listening for Him. Then, once you're listening, the question is

Are you hearing His intent

Taking the words to heart

Do you hear what He's saying?

The Bible tells us about a man who learned to listen for the whisper. Elijah. Thankfully, the Bible also tells us that Elijah was a man just like us.[7] In Elijah's encounter with God, we read:

Then He said, "Go out, and stand on the mountain before the LORD." And behold, the LORD passed by, and a great and strong wind tore into the mountains and broke the rocks in pieces before the LORD, but the LORD was not in the wind; and after the wind an earthquake, but the LORD was not in the earthquake; and after the earthquake a fire, but the LORD was not in the fire; and after the fire a still small voice.[8]

So often we want God to speak to us in some miraculous extravaganza, but He just wants to talk to us. And while we're listening for the big bang of fireworks, we miss the still, small voice.

This is a lesson I learned with my children as well. One day, I was shouting for them. Not because I was mad, but I didn't want to stop what I was doing, go to where they were and talk. So I yelled, *"Hey, everyone! C'mere!"* Immediately, *I* heard a still, small voice.

"Stop it." I knew it was the Lord.

"Stop it?" I asked.

"Yes. Stop yelling. If your children don't learn to hear your still, small voice, they will never be able to hear Mine." *They would always be listening for the shout.*

I stopped yelling.

"He who has an ear, let him hear what the Spirit says to the churches."

We are all tempted to "yell" at people, even without our voice. Sometimes yelling can be the cold shoulder or icy silence or non-response. Sometimes yelling is talking over the other person and not listening. How often have we hindered relationships because we don't listen? We get defensive. We try to explain ourselves, to give a reason for our actions, to convince of the purity of our motive. And maybe our motives were pure. But that isn't what's needed. What is really needed is for us to

Hear. Listen. Pay attention. Perceive. Observe. Understand.
Know them better because we hear their heart.

Often our hesitance to listen is due to the fact that we have been stung by the words of people in the past. All of us communicate so inadequately and incompletely. James warns us of the destructive power of our words,[9] and the book of Proverbs tells us that the power of life and death are in our words.[10] Yes—we've all been stung.

With our Bridegroom, Jesus, we never need to worry. His words are always for our good. Scripture defines the words of God as pure,[11] creative,[12] healing,[13] and life-giving.[14] When He speaks, even firmly, His words are always intended to heal us, make us new, give life, instill His purity in us.

But we have to listen.

Scott and I had a communication rule in our relationship. I suppose that it could be called the "benefit of the doubt" rule. We agreed that we would give each other the benefit of the doubt that we didn't intend to be mean or hurt each other. Of course, that meant we had to choose not to be mean or push the other's buttons. But even though I tried not to, did I say things that came across as mean? Yup. Didn't intend to. But I did. Did I hurt his feelings? Yup. Didn't intend to. But I did.

But with the "benefit of the doubt" rule, we would talk it out, rephrase and work on it until we were sure we had heard each other's hearts. Jesus now asks us for the same consideration. He's asking us to trust that His words are always for our good.

He's asking us to listen.

To respond. To act.

To change direction.

Hear what the Spirit is saying . . .

I have always loved how *THE MESSAGE* version interprets Revelation 2:7: "Are your ears awake? Listen. Listen to the Wind Words, the Spirit blowing through the churches." Many of us know that in both of the original languages of Scripture, the words translated "Spirit" can also be translated "breath" or "wind." In the Bible, we see God breathe into Adam, and he became a living being.[15] Jesus breathed on His disciples in the Upper Room and new life was theirs.[16] Today, Jesus has given us His Holy Spirit so that we can hear His voice,[17] and He calls to His Church, to His Bride, to you, to me . . .

Hear what the Spirit says to the churches.
Still, small voice. Wind words. Listen for the whispers.

---

1. John 16:33.
2. Matthew 16:24-25.
3. 1 Corinthians 15:55, author's paraphrase.
4. Luke 24:5, author's paraphrase.
5. John 12:24.
6. Revelation 21:2-5.
7. See James 5:17.
8. 1 Kings 19:11-12.
9. See James 3:5-6.
10. See Proverbs 18:21.
11. See Psalm 12:6.
12. See Psalm 33:6.
13. See Psalm 107:20.
14. See Psalm 119:50.
15. See Genesis 2:7.
16. See John 20:22.
17. See John 16:13.

Encountering Him

ARE YOUR EARS AWAKE?

Learning how to hear God takes practice. In fact, I once spoke to a women's group and asked a question about hearing God. One woman replied, "I've never heard God."

Well, she has . . . she just didn't know it was Him. I know that, because He speaks to all of us. But it takes practice to recognize Him. We also each have preconceived notions of how the Lord is going to speak to us. Or we want Him to speak to us like He speaks to our friend or to our pastor.

But God deals with each one of us as individuals, and He speaks to us that way too. For example, I'm very visual—I love art, painting and drawing. So it's unsurprising to me that God would often speak to me in pictures. Pictures aren't an unusual way for God to show us things. We see it all over Scripture![1]

Okay . . . before you decide I've gone off of the deep end, let me give you two guidelines for hearing God that I believe are inviolable.

First, God speaks most often through His Word and will not tell you anything that conflicts with what is in the Bible. It is our absolute guideline. So if you believe God has told you something that the Bible doesn't support, forget it! That wasn't Him.

Second, I believe that the thing that most often hinders us from hearing the Lord is sin in our life. And we've all got it. Sin, that is. Whether we like it or not, we fall miserably on our faces again and again.

The good news is that "He remembers that we are dust." Our Father in heaven loves us and is infinitely patient with us. Let me give you an example. As I write, I have three one-year-old grandsons who are all learning to walk. Today, no one expects them to walk perfectly. They're just learning. No one in our family is going to get angry with them because they fall down. Rather, we run over, steady them on their feet and encourage them to try again. Keep on going. Keep on trying.

I believe that is how the Father is with us. We beat ourselves up that we aren't perfect and that we've fallen down again, but He is right there cheering us on to try again.

Admittedly, if I had a five-year-old grandchild who hadn't mastered walking, there would be something very wrong. But we still wouldn't be mad at that child. We'd be trying to resolve the issue.

Again, I believe that is how the Father is with us.

All to say that sin (and its effects) is an issue in our lives that won't be completely resolved until we get to heaven. But dealing with it, cutting out known sin in our lives and continuing to press forward all help to keep our ears clean, so to speak, and allow us to hear the Lord at ever-increasing levels.

So how do you hear God?

The Bible talks about a number of ways that the Lord speaks to people.

First, a big one is through nature. In fact, Scripture says that not only does nature inspire praise in God's people, but it can also draw the hearts of unbelievers toward Him—draw them to begin to seek for the one who is the maker of all things.[2] And Scripture promises that when people begin to seek Him, they *will* find Him.

Second, in the Word, God spoke to many people in dreams. Take the circumstances surrounding Jesus' birth. Joseph was obviously a man who heard God in dreams. And please—not every dream is from the Lord! Some are from that cold pizza you ate before you went to bed. Be discerning!

Third, for me, a big one is "suddenly knowing what to do." I don't kid myself—I can't do my life successfully or well without God's involvement in it. When I don't know what to do, I pray. And so do you. But how often do we suddenly know what to do and forget to recognize or thank the Lord for His involvement in the process? In my own experience, I would say that about 95 percent of the time, I have found those moments to be God at work, helping me with life.

And the more I ask, the more He speaks!

Why do we need to ask? Why can't He just lead us anyway?

I believe that it is important to ask because it requires a continual attitude of humility to come before the Lord on matters big and small, acknowledging that "if You don't help me, I can't do this."

Fourth, He speaks through His Word, His Word, His Word! Yes . . . back to His Word! I love the Bible, and I encourage every believer to read it each day, to commit it to heart and to keep growing in the knowledge of what God has revealed. It is *the* measure for every part of life.

Our tendency is to make hearing from God a spooky or mysterious process instead of simply hearing from Him as a natural part of our lives. So today, can I encourage you to ask the Lord to speak to you? Start by getting out your Bible and reading until a verse speaks to your heart.

You can stop with that or go on to more study. Get out your concordance and look up other Scriptures on that same topic or ones that have a similar wording. Identify why a verse spoke to you. How does it apply to your life? What is one step you are going to take *today* because the Lord spoke that verse to you? Jot down what He's said in a journal. And let me say again: I encourage every believer to spend time in the Word every day. As you do, you'll begin to see an increased flow of Jesus speaking to your heart.

Revelation calls us to "hear what the Spirit is saying to the churches." That's Him, and that's us . . . and He has a lot to say to His Bride!

---

1. Zechariah 4:2 and Acts 10:9-16, just to name two.
2. See Psalm 19:1; Romans 1:20.

rebecca hayford bauer · www.regalbooks.com

CAUGHT UP WITH HIM

When I was a little girl my parents taught me to pray each night before I went to bed. Beyond the "now I lay me down to sleep" type of prayers, they taught me to pray for people and situations—my very first lessons in intercession.

Though not lengthy, my bedtime prayers generally went something like this:

> *Dear Jesus,*
>
> *Bless Mommy and Daddy, and Jack, Mark and Chris. Bless Gramma and Grampa Hayford, and Gramma and Grampa Smith. Bless all of the missionaries and help them tell a lot of people about You. Help me at school. Help me to be a good girl. And help me to be ready when You come.*
>
> *In Jesus' name, amen.*

Wrapped in that little prayer were lessons that have helped me my whole life:

> Living a spiritual life begins at home
> > Stay busy with the harvest
> > > I always need help
> > > > Keep my focus on eternity

Now and Then

"Being ready for Jesus to come" can actually be a scary thought when you're a kid. I remember being afraid that He would come back too soon. "I don't want Jesus to come yet! I want to get married and have kids." Well—I've done those things, and now the next generation is getting married and having kids. And guess what—I want to be around for that too.

Another big fear I remember was simply—What if I don't go when He comes? I remember reading (and completely misunderstanding) certain Scriptures and being terrified! One was:

I tell you, on that night there will be two in one bed; one will be taken and the other will be left. There will be two women grinding at the same place; one will be taken and the other will be left. Two men will be in the field; one will be taken and the other will be left.[1]

I honestly thought in my childish understanding that I needed to always make sure to sleep by myself because I thought it was automatic: when Jesus came back only one person would go. I thought that even if you both loved and served Jesus, He would still only pick one. I was really nervous about Mom and Dad sharing a bed! Of course, I later learned that wasn't true, but the fear still persisted. What if I thought I was ready and wasn't?

What if I didn't go when He came back?

My dad was no different. He faced that fear as a young teen. It was 1948, and Israel—often referred to as God's prophetic timepiece—had just become a nation. Many believers were talking about the possibility of Jesus' soon return. As he processed all of this, his own concerns grew. Finally one day, he went to his mother and asked, "How can I be sure that I will be caught up in the Rapture when Jesus comes again?"

My grandmother was a very wise woman, and after a bit of thought she told him:

Those who are caught up with Him *now*
Are those who will be caught up with Him *then*.

As we've walked through this book together, we have seen over and over how Jesus longs for His people to be passionate about Him—as passionate as He is about them. We use the term "Rapture" to describe Jesus' coming, and, in fact, "rapture" has a very passionate definition. It means "an expression or manifestation of ecstasy or passion; a state or experience of being carried away by overwhelming emotion."[2] When Jesus comes to rapture us—to catch us away—it will be because of His overwhelming love for us; and He desires a Bride that is equally in love with Him. It's what "caught up with Him" looks like.

Overwhelming love. Passion. Rapture.

Always Ready

We've learned already that during the betrothal period the bride was to diligently be ready at all times. But think about what the practical reality of this may have been.

Can you imagine the betrothed bride going to bed each night not knowing if *that* would be the night her bridegroom would come?

For months.

And she had to be constantly ready for that possibility. I'll bet she never forgot her beauty routine! I'll bet she never skipped her shower. Each night, her clothes were laid out, her hair done, her skin smoothed with ointment.

In case.

Or every time she went to the central town market—the possibility existed that she could turn the corner and there he would be, suddenly coming down the street to sweep her away. She could be paying a call to a friend, or taking lunch to her dad in the field, or getting water from the well—and he could appear.

Any moment could be *THE* moment!

It's how we're called to live. The Bible calls it "loving His appearing." And it comes with a promise that He will put the final adorning touch to our preparation.

> *There is reserved for me a crown of righteousness . . .*
> *Not to me only but also to all who have loved His appearing.*[3]

> *He has covered me with the robe of righteousness,*
> *As a bridegroom decks himself with ornaments,*
> *And as a bride adorns herself with her jewels.*[4]

He's Coming Today

Jesus is coming back! He will physically come again to earth; He will catch away His Bride; and He will establish His rule.

But until then, He wants to come to us every day. Not only are we looking for His appearing when it's time for the wedding, but we are also to look for His guidance, His presence, His direction and words of love

every day.

There are three ways that He does that.

First, He comes by His Spirit. He promised that He wouldn't leave us alone but would send a Helper. Until He comes again, He has left His Spirit to lead, guide and strengthen us. He is there to help us to do our lives well—in a way that honors and glorifies our Bridegroom and King.

A mom at one of my sons' baseball games once described to me how God had helped her with one of her kids. The action the Lord had told her to take had such a profound effect on her child that there was no denying that God had moved on her behalf. He had basically given her a "word of knowledge," as the apostle described in 1 Corinthians 12:8.

What made me chuckle to myself is that she would never have described it that way, because she didn't believe in "the gifts of the Holy Spirit." Yet, despite our doctrinal opinions and shortcomings (and we've all got them), God looks on hearts that love Him and He helps us anyway. However she would or would not have described what happened, Jesus came to her that day.

Just like He wants to come to us every day. Jesus said:

I will pray the Father, and He will give you another Helper, that He may abide with you forever—the Spirit of truth, whom the world cannot receive . . . but you know Him, for He dwells with you and will be in you. I will not leave you orphans; I will come to you.[5]

He also comes to us in the Word—speaking to us and teaching us from Scripture. The Bible is the measure for everything we do. It's why it is so important for us to be in the Word—all of it, Old and New Testaments. "The whole counsel of God" is profitable for doctrine, for reproof, for correction, for instruction in righteousness.[6] We should be encouraged to be in the Word more—studying, reading, learning—because how can He speak to us through the Word if we're not in it?

This Book of the Law shall not depart from your mouth,
but you shall meditate in it day and night,
that you may observe to do according to all that is written in it.
For then you will make your way prosperous,
and then you will have good success.[7]

Desire the pure milk of the word, that you may grow thereby.[8]

The third way Jesus comes to us every day is through His Body—other brothers and sisters in Christ. Those "comings" are opportunities we often miss because we are in the middle of our own busy lives, and we just hurry by. But we miss giving and receiving so many ministry moments that could build us up, and build up the people around us. Jesus even went so far as to say that our ministry to one another, even the simplest offering of a cup of water, is ministering to Him.

> He who receives you receives Me, and he who receives Me receives Him who sent Me. He who receives a prophet in the name of a prophet shall receive a prophet's reward. And he who receives a righteous man in the name of a righteous man shall receive a righteous man's reward. And whoever gives one of these little ones only a cup of cold water in the name of a disciple, assuredly, I say to you, he shall by no means lose his reward.[9]

Ask the Lord to help you see His comings and hear His voice by His Spirit, in His Word, and in the Church, because

He wants to come to us every day.

Watching and Waiting

The betrothed bride may have seen her bridegroom every day, too, just like Jesus wants to come to us every day. Did she ever see her beloved across the marketplace? Or as she passed the shop where he worked? Or helping his mother up the steps at synagogue? She could see him every day, even though it wasn't *the* day. But she was watching! All the time.

A woman once asked me, "Jesus hasn't come yet, and we've been waiting for 2,000 years. Why should I think He's going to come now?" She wasn't the first one to ask that question. In fact, Peter addressed it less than 40 years after Jesus' death and resurrection. He wrote this comforting and encouraging reminder to watch:

> Beloved, do not forget this one thing, that with the Lord one day is as a thousand years, and a thousand years as one day. The Lord is not slack concerning His promise, as some count

slackness, but is longsuffering toward us, not willing that any should perish but that all should come to repentance. But the day of the Lord will come as a thief in the night . . . Therefore . . . what manner of persons ought you to be in holy conduct and godliness, looking for and hastening the coming of the day of God.[10]

We are called to always live in expectancy; we watch for His comings every day, and we await the rapture of His return. In the process, we grow more in love with Him as time goes by. The wedding isn't far away!

Love Letter

The joy of loving you grows with every year. I know more about you. I share more of myself with you. I discover new dimensions of our life together. Nothing compares to the joy that you bring me. Nothing compares to the trust and confidence I have in your love. You are a gift from God . . . I am very thankful that we are us!

sgb to rlb
Valentine's Day 1992

Jesus' first miracle was at a wedding—attending to a detail that made *that* couple's celebration perfect.[11] In doing so, He looked forward to the day that He would receive *His* Bride to Himself. Jesus is walking the process and invites us to do the same, as together we look forward to the fulfillment of His return and the celebration of the marriage supper.

Even so come quickly, Lord Jesus!
I'm caught up with You.

---

1. Luke 17:34-36, *NASB*.
2. "Rapture," *Merriam-Webster*. http://www.merriam-webster.com/dictionary/rapture.
3. 2 Timothy 4:8, author's paraphrase.
4. Isaiah 61:10.
5. John 14:16-18.
6. See Acts 20:27; 2 Timothy 3:16.
7. Joshua 1:8.
8. 1 Peter 2:2.
9. Matthew 10:40-42.
10. 2 Peter 3:8-12.
11. See John 2:1-12.

Encountering Him

LETTER TO THE LORD

Have you ever written a letter to the Lord? At the church I go to, every New Year's Eve we have a service when we write a letter to Him about the coming year—what we would like to see Him accomplish in our lives, what He's speaking to us about, how much we love Him. Then we receive the Lord's Table together. It's a very sweet time of communion with Him and with other believers.

Throughout this book, we've talked about the Lord's love letters to us. Now I'm going to invite you to write a love letter to Him. I have already described a yearly time that I write a letter to Him, but what is involved in writing a love letter to the Lord? Allow me to give you a couple of guidelines and an example.

Getting Ready to Write

I'm a very visual person, so I like to write in a beautiful place. What's beautiful to me may not be the same for you. There isn't a right or wrong answer to this. You may like to write outside. Someone I know uses her car as a place to get away. She can use it on a break at work or during the kids' soccer practice, and it still provides a confined, personal space for her. What works for you? Whatever it is, choose a place to write that's comfortable and inviting so that you can focus on what you want to say to Jesus.

Typically, a love letter is written on beautiful paper. When I write to the Lord, I like to write in my journal. The paper is thick, creamy and smooth, and the book it's in is beautiful too. I also like to write with a favorite pen that glides over the paper rather than with something that skips and advertises dog food on the side.

What Do I Write About?

A love letter might include remembering when you met. What were the circumstances that brought you to the Lord and to salvation?

Talk about how your life has changed for the better because He is in it. Recall special times of worship or provision or healing. You might write a Scripture verse that has been special to you. What are the qualities that you especially love about the Lord? Then reaffirm your love and commitment to Him.

Writing to the Lord helps us to remember, and Scripture talks a lot about remembering. One of my favorite books is Deuteronomy, in which the Lord calls His people again and again to remember from where He brought them, to remember His mighty works and to remember His commandments. The psalms call us to "Remember His marvelous works which He has done, His wonders, and the judgments of His mouth."[1] But perhaps one of the most poignant verses in Scripture is Nehemiah 9:17. The entire chapter rehearses the wilderness wanderings of Israel, and the attitudes of the people: pride, hardness of heart, rebellion, even wanting to return to bondage. And then the reason for all of those attitudes is revealed: "They were not mindful of [His] wonders."

I don't ever want to forget the wonders the Lord has done in my life, His faithfulness, provision and love. Revelation 12:11 tells us that God's people overcome by the blood of the Lamb (our salvation), and by the word of their testimony. Writing down God's kindnesses helps me to remember. Meditating on His wonders keeps my testimony fresh and alive. Rehearsing those things engraves them on my heart.

Sample Letter

Dear Lord Jesus,

How I love You! How I thank You for all You've done in my life! How I can't live without You! I could not take a step or breathe a breath without You. Thank You. Thank You that You love me.

Today I want to thank You for how present You were when I had to walk through the valley of the shadow. It was so dark . . . yet You never left my side. I weep even as I write, because You held my hand so tightly and even carried me when I was sure I couldn't take another step.

Not only did You walk me through the darkest days of my life, but You have walked me into a beautiful future that I could not have imagined! Thank You for Your redemption. Thank You for healing my heart. Thank You that in You there is—and always will be—a future and a hope.

Thank You for Your kindness when I am hurting. Thank You for sharing the joy of my heart. Thank You for confronting me when I need to grow up or change my attitude. Thank You for always pressing me to become more than I am. One of my favorite verses reminds me that You have laid hold of me for a purpose.[2] Thank You that You give meaning to my life, and purpose to my future.

Jesus, I love You. Help me to be ready for Your coming; help me to love Your appearing. Help me to continually be becoming the Bride without spot or wrinkle. I want to be that for You. I want to be everything You want me to be. I want to be everything You see in me.

I am—and always will be—Yours, and I ask that You help me to continually be caught up with You now, so that I'm caught up with You then,

Rebecca

---

1. Psalm 105:5.
2. See Philippians 3:12.

Group Discussion Questions

Group Discussion Questions

An Introduction: Love Letters

1. Describe a time when God's love has been evident in your life—this can be as simple as a time you simply felt His love, or a time that you experienced a miracle, or a time that a door opened that allowed you to bless someone else.

2. Read 1 Corinthians 13 together. What characteristic of love stands out the most to you? Which characteristic do you think people would see most in your life? Which characteristic do you think you most need to work on?

3. Is it difficult or easy to see yourself as part of the Bride of Christ? Why?

4. How will you accept His invitation to "rise up, My love, My fair one, and come away"? We can give mental assent to an idea, or actually make room for it in our lives. This may mean time in the Word or prayer. It may mean working on one of the "love" characteristics mentioned in 1 Corinthians 13. Whatever your response, it should require some kind of tangible action on your part. So, again . . . how will you accept His invitation?

5. What words come to mind to describe what you would like this journey with Jesus to look like? Feel like? Change in your life?

The Purpose of the Process: First Comes Love

1. Have you encountered a "teaching moment" recently—something that you shared with someone else? Something from your pastor's sermon? Something that a friend helped you learn? Describe that moment and how it has impacted your life.

2. We looked at the process that Jesus is walking as an engaged man waiting to receive His Bride. How does knowing that there is a process and that He is honoring it change your understanding of *our* waiting time here on earth?

3. We know that we're not only walking a process, but we're all "in process" too. What is the Lord doing in your life right now that is growing you into a "Bride without spot or wrinkle"?

4. Part of the bride's responsibility during the betrothal period was the *mikvah*. Have you been baptized in water? If so, what led you to make that decision? If not, what has kept you from it? (Maybe you were baptized as an infant, or you never knew that it was something that Jesus directed His disciples to do. Look at these Scriptures to see Jesus' words on the topic: Matthew 28:19 and Mark 16:16. Jesus also modeled baptism for us (see Matthew 3:13-16). It was also clearly practiced by the Early Church (see Acts 2:38), and Paul writes that it is symbolic of our death and resurrection with Christ (see Romans 6:3-4).

5. In this week's Encounter, we talked about worship. What is the most recent song you purchased or downloaded, and what do you think it says about you and your life's focus?

May I Introduce You: Meet Him Again

1. Has there ever been a time when you made an assumption about someone that you found out later was completely untrue? Tell about that experience. How did that change how you form opinions about people?

2. How did you view God when you were a child? How has that view affected how you view Him today? Do you need to "meet Him again" in that part of your relationship with Him?

3. What surprised you most about the idea that Mary and John had to "meet Jesus again"?

4. Isaiah 35:10 talks about what happens when we return to the Lord: singing, joy and gladness. "And sorrow and sighing shall flee away." Is there any place in your life that you need to turn your back on "sorrow and sighing" and return to the Lord? What is that area? What has held you back from returning to the Lord regarding that specific issue?

5. Which of the four "roles" of Jesus—Igniter, Confronter, Protector, Completer—spoke to you? Why?

To the Church at Ephesus . . . The Passion

1. What does the word "passion" evoke in your mind when you hear it? Is it possible to feel love without passion? How are passion and love different? The same?

2. Is there an area of your walk with the Lord that you have allowed responsibility to overtake your passion for Him? Where does passion need to be renewed?

3. On page 72, Kenda Creasy Dean's story about "heading towards the farm, or away from it" is related. Are there any areas in your life where you need to turn the other way and head back toward Jesus? What steps can you take today to begin that process?

4. What attributes of God thrill your heart?

5. Share about your salvation encounter with Jesus. What led up to it? How did He woo your heart?

To the Church at Smyrna . . . The Choice

1. What are the criteria on which you base your choices? How do we base our choices on more than just emotion, yet not dismiss emotion entirely?

2. Are there things you consciously do to "choose Jesus every day"? What are they? (For example, a friend briefly kneels by his bed each morning to acknowledge that Jesus is Lord as the day begins. For others, regular Bible reading may signify that choice. Another friend asks the Lord each morning what she should wear, recognizing that everywhere she goes she is representing Him first.) If you don't have anything like this in your life right now, is there something you would like to start doing on a daily basis to signify this choice?

3. What characteristics attract you to people? How do you see those same characteristics in Jesus? What "attracted" you to Him?

4. What is one thing in your life in which you struggle making the right choice? What are some practical and accountable steps that you can take to overcome in this area? When everyone has shared, pray together for the Lord's strength in the challenges that each one faces.

5. Rebecca writes, "The good news is that character is learned. Character is practiced. Character is chosen." Name one area in your life where you are choosing to grow in character. What is the best measurable indicator that you are growing in that area?

To the Church at Laodicea . . . The Proposal

1. If you are married, tell about your proposal. What details made it special and unique to you and your spouse? If you are single, share how you think you would like a proposal to take place. Why would that be special to you?

2. What have you thought when you have heard "hot" and "cold" in this passage of Scripture? What do you think about the need for both "fire" and "water" in your life, and in your walk with the Lord?

3. Discuss the idea of being complete in Christ. Have you ever tried to find a person to "complete" you? Describe that situation. How did it turn out? How does Jesus bring completion to your life? Tell about one way that He has done that.

4. In this chapter, we talked about the fact that true love will confront. Is there anything that God has confronted you about? How have you responded? Did you follow through on what the Lord asked you to do? What three changes in you would please God most? Why? Are you submitting to the leadership of the Bridegroom? Where do you need to say yes to Him?

5. Tell about a special meal that you've had—and not every special meal is a big deal; it may just be at a diner having burgers. What was the situation or celebration? What happened?

To the Church at Pergamos . . . The Diamond

1. There were several definitions given of "fully engaged." Which one spoke to you? Why? How does it describe what the Lord is doing in your life?

2. Has there ever been an "idol" in your life? In this chapter, we looked at the fact that anything can become an idol—from the most intimate relationship in your life to the most trivial thing that you own. When you recognized that that person or thing had become an idol, what did you do about it?

3. How does how you spend your money show "where your treasure is"? Have you ever been challenged by the Lord in how you spend your money? In how you give?

4. What are some of the characteristics of diamonds? Discuss how those characteristics are applicable in a marriage or other relationship. How are those characteristics applicable in your relationship with the Lord?

5. What has God told you about your future? How is "your future bigger than your past"? Realizing that God has a bigger plan for your life, where do you see yourself at this same time next year? What about five years from now?

To the Church at Sardis . . . The Gown

1. Think about how you would want to dress to meet Jesus. When you have thought about it, would it make a difference if you stood before Him with what you have on right now? Do you think He would even care about what you're wearing? Why or why not?

2. The Bible tells us that God is clothed with salvation, majesty, strength and honor, to say nothing of how Jesus was dressed when He met John in Revelation 1! With the knowledge of how He is dressed, and the understanding that He "covers us" with *His garment*, what does that say to you about the provision of His clothing for us? (See 2 Chronicles 6:41, Psalms 93:1; 104:1.)

3. The concept of God covering us and being our "kinsman-redeemer" (like Boaz) promises us protection, acceptance, redemption and provision. Is there one of these areas that you need provision for?

4. Standing before the Lord made Isaiah "see" himself—showing up the areas of his life that needed the Lord's touch. Is there a place that you need the Lord's touch in your life today?

5. Jesus told a parable about women who were prepared to meet the bridegroom and women who were not. And we know that culturally, the bride was to be in a continual state of readiness. How are you getting ready to meet the Bridegroom?

To the Church at Philadelphia . . . The Name

1. Did you ever wish you had a different name? What was it? What did you like about it? Have you ever asked God to give you a new

name? If so, how did He answer you? If not, do you think that is something that would help further your walk and growth in the Lord?

2. Are there names that you have been called that are stuck in your head? They are lies, you know. Whatever they are, or however true they may have been at another time in your life, the Lord is continually at work, changing and growing us. The Bible says that He is always taking us "from glory to glory" (2 Corinthians 3:18). Today, in boldness and in the safety of other believers, take one of those names and boldly renounce it.

3. After you have all done this, join hands together and pray for the Lord to remove those names from your heart and their whispers from your mind. Remember, He makes all things new.

4. What is a name of God in Scripture that is special to you? Share the story of how that name impacted your life.

5. What do you call Jesus?

To the Church at Thyatira . . . The Partnership

1. List all of the partnerships in your life. These could be personal, business, family, financial, friendships. How are you nurturing the positive partnerships in your life? On the other hand, are there any partnerships that should not be there? Are there friendships that compromise you that should be removed from your life? Are there steps that can be taken to turn these into godly partnerships?

2. Have you ever tried to fulfill God's Word in your life instead of waiting for Him to do it? What happened?

3. How would your life change if you viewed yourself like Jesus sees you? As you see yourself as Jesus' beloved, partner, bride—how does that enlarge your view of His purpose and call in your life?

4. Ask yourself: If someone were my friend, what should they know about me? How does that make me see my uniqueness in the eyes of God? Have I ever talked to Jesus about how He would like for me to use that in my life?

5. Second Corinthians 3:3 tells us that we are "an epistle of Christ" . . . we carry His message everywhere we go. What is the message of Christ that your life tells to the people around you?

Listen for the Whispers: Sweet Somethings

1. How does it make you feel to know that Jesus "knows your works"? Does that feel intimidating or comforting? Why?

2. Are there any works in your life that should change? What are they? What step could you take right now that would move you closer to your goal?

3. Who are the people in your life who are your cheerleaders? What do they do that keeps you reaching forward?

4. What tribulation have you faced and overcome?

5. How do you hear the Lord? Share a time when the Lord uniquely spoke to you. I'm not necessarily talking about a "thus sayeth the Lord" moment, but as John Wesley once described—his "heart was strangely warmed," and he knew it was the Lord making His presence real.

This Could Be the Day: Caught Up with Him

1. How do you delight in the Lord? What does being "caught up with Him" look like in your life?

2. How has Jesus "come" to you this week?

3. When you think about the return of Jesus Christ . . . what do you think of? Does the thought excite you? Scare you? Scripture calls us to "love His appearing." What does that phrase say to you?

4. How has this book made you view the letters in Revelation differently? What was your biggest surprise in reading them from a "love letter" viewpoint?

5. What specific thing have you learned by reading this book? What are some applications you can make in your personal life? Which chapter was the most difficult for you? Why? Which chapter was most life-changing?

About the Author

In ministry for more than 30 years, Rebecca Bauer has a passion to see people integrate what they believe into their everyday lives. "After all," she says, "if you can't take your theology home and live it, what's the point?" The living out of this passion has taken many forms, including speaking both nationally and internationally, as well as teaching at The King's University and at Foursquare Ignite Academy, a discipleship school for high school graduates. She received her theological training at Life Bible College (1979) and Regent University (2002) and is a certified life coach (2008).

Rebecca has three children (all married), nine (and counting!) grandchildren, and was married for 27 years to Pastor Scott Bauer. The dark valley of Rebecca's life came when Scott suddenly died in 2003 of a brain aneurysm. "Life as I knew it was over," she says. Walking that journey, however, has taught Rebecca that God's promises are the real deal. Jeremiah 32:44 says, "I [the Lord] will make everything as good for them as it once was" (NCV). "I have found that to be true!" says Rebecca. "As incredible as it sounds . . . God makes life good again after tragedy, He makes all things new, and it really is *as good as it once was!*"

In her spare time, Rebecca can be found enjoying nachos, the color orange, long walks, and of course, all of those grandkids! Current projects include starting back to school, and developing "women's only" Israel tours focusing on meeting Jesus as the Bridegroom.

Rebecca can be contacted at:
RebeccaBauer.org

Follow Rebecca at:
Twitter.com/bauerrebecca

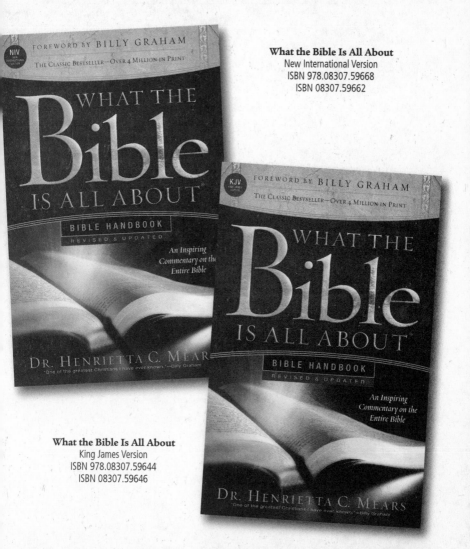

GOD IS SPEAKING . . . WILL YOU LISTEN?

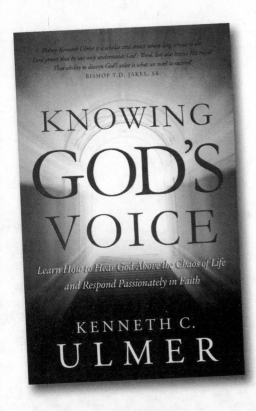

Knowing God's Voice
Kenneth C. Ulmer
ISBN 978.08307.58906
ISBN 08307.58909

Healthy give-and-take relationships do not happen when one person does all the talking—so why do so many Christians forget to let God get a word in edgewise? If you're like many believers, you may not know how to listen for and respond in faith to the voice of God. But now, in *Knowing God's Voice*, Dr. Kenneth C. Ulmer shows you how to hear from God and act on His words. It may be difficult sometimes, in the midst of all that you are facing, to feel confident that the Almighty takes a personal interest in your life. *Knowing God's Voice* is the assurance you have been waiting for: God is interested, and He has a lot to say in return! In these pages, you will learn to discern God's voice from the background noise of internal anxiety and external circumstances, and to trust His guidance and revelation even in trying times. God is speaking to His people, if only we will have ears to hear!